PRAISE FOR
GOD'S PEOPLE MADE NEW

"With passion, insight, and wisdom, Powell offers a compelling testimony to the power of proclaiming the biblical story. She demonstrates how the Spirit works when the church does two simple things—asks a good question and turns to the Bible with open hearts."

> —Rolf Jacobson, professor of Old Testament
> and Alvin N. Rogness Chair of Scripture,
> Theology, and Ministry, Luther Seminary

"Honest. Inspiring. Practical. These are the words that best capture Rachael Powell's *God's People Made New*. Placing her pastoral experience alongside the insights of philosophers from Aristotle to Paul Ricoeur, Powell articulates her conviction that the biblical story has the power to gather and transform the stories of our lives, our congregations, and our world. Deeply rooted in Scripture, animated by honest reflection on our calling as preachers, and filled with practical counsel derived from her own experience, Powell's writing probes and celebrates the transformation we can expect when we allow God's Word to breathe new life and purpose into God's people."

> —David J. Lose, senior pastor of Mount Olivet
> Lutheran Church, Minneapolis, Minnesota;
> former president of the Lutheran Theological
> Seminary at Philadelphia; and author of
> *Preaching at the Crossroads: How the World—and
> Our Preaching—Is Changing* (Fortress, 2013)

"*God's People Made New* is the honest, engaging, and ultimately hope-filled story of one congregation's journey through death to resurrection. Their story is a witness to the power of the Holy Spirit, who forms them as a people as they find their identity in the pages of Scripture. What a simple yet profound testimony: the Word of God equips the people of God to be about God's mission in the world! The story of Grace Church will inspire hope for all who read it."

—Kathryn Schifferdecker, professor and
Elva B. Lovell Chair of Old Testament, Luther Seminary

"In this incredibly timely and accessible work, Powell weaves together the centrality of scriptural narrative and our real-life experience as the church, turning our gaze from our own efforts to God, who never fails to bring new life from death. Taking seriously *God's People Made New* will help reframe every conversation we are having about the future of Christ's church."

—Jim Gonia, bishop, Rocky Mountain Synod,
Evangelical Lutheran Church in America

GOD'S PEOPLE
MADE NEW

GOD'S

PEOPLE

MADE NEW

How Exploring the Bible Together Launched a
Church's Spirit-Filled Future

RACHAEL J. POWELL

FORTRESS PRESS
Minneapolis

GOD'S PEOPLE MADE NEW
How Exploring the Bible Together Launched a Church's Spirit-Filled Future

Cover Image: 482762483 © johnwoodcock | iStock
Cover Design: Marti Naughton

Print ISBN: 978-1-5064-6705-4
eBook ISBN: 978-1-5064-6706-1

To God Be the Glory

CONTENTS

PREFACE

Two months into my first call as a pastor, I was required to attend a "First Call Theological Training." All pastors who had been serving congregations for three years or less were cordially required to be there. The national church body was a bit worried about the attrition rate of pastors in their first three years and had begun to offer these trainings to support pastors during this vulnerable time. I didn't realize it then, but I was the poster child for this event.

The long and short of it is I was a mess. I had been working about fifteen hours a day. I was at the church before the sun came up and long after it had set. From my current vantage point, seventeen years later, I realize I was trying to prove to my congregation that they didn't make a mistake by hiring a pastor so young and with no experience. In reality, I was trying to prove to myself and, if I'm honest, to God that my call to ministry wasn't a catastrophic error.

I was more than a little grumpy arriving at the retreat center where the three-day event was held. I couldn't fathom having to be away from the daily operations of my congregation. I had way too many things to do there to be spending my time retreating here, or so I thought. I found my room, set down my overnight bag, and dutifully headed to the conference center for the first evening session. Only three people beat me there. I was an overachiever, a perfectionist type, and I prided myself on arriving at least fifteen minutes early to everything. In uncharacteristic fashion, I let my irritation get the best of me and asked the three people, "So who else doesn't want to be here?" An awkward silence followed. Soon after, about forty more pastors filed in, and we were given a few brief introductions. Finally, we met our featured speaker. He, of course, was one of the three people who had heard my clear confession that I wished I wasn't in attendance. I was off to a wonderful start.

But after his first plenary session, we heard from a local pastor who had been serving in a congregational setting for some time. She was smart, direct, and insightful. She said something that made an impact in the moment but that I wouldn't understand fully until a decade or so later. Mission statements had just begun to make a splash among churches, and my own congregation was going through a process to determine one for themselves. In her opinion, mission statements were good and helpful for focusing a congregation's ministry where they were planted. But then she said, "Just remember, no matter what your church decides regarding your specific mission statement, God already has a mission, and that mission has a church: *thy kingdom come.*" Instantly, I felt the semi that had been parked on my chest for the last two months lift. It felt so grace filled to imagine that the church was about *God's mission* and not something we had to determine. Could it be true that *God* would set the agenda for our congregation and that we didn't have to figure it out? Was it possible that I could set aside all those books I'd been reading about mission plans and population studies and just ask God what God would have us do?

God had opened the door for me to catch a glimpse of what the church in God's world was all about, but I wasn't anywhere near ready. I had years and years of experience as an achiever. I believed that everything worth doing required hard work, tenacity, sweat from my brow, and callouses on my hands. The church wasn't God's project; it was ours! I had no time to lose! I had church growth books to read and mission development seminars to attend. My congregation was looking to me for leadership, and by God, I would give it to them!

In retrospect, I know we did some incredibly beautiful ministry together, my first call church and I. But most of it was because of God's patience with me and the faithfulness of the people I served.

What I know now is that all of my diligent study and countless hours at church were important and, ultimately, necessary. I needed to do all of that work in order for God to show me that it wasn't my work that would move the church. It wasn't the wisdom of brilliant scholars and my ability to inwardly digest their writings that would re-create God's people over and over again in order that we would thrive. The only one who could do all of this and so much more was and is God. What I understand fully at this moment is that I am called to read, to study, to learn, and to work diligently for the sake of the gospel. I am given the gifts of scholarly perspectives and theological treatises to expand my understanding of who *God* is as Creator, Savior, and Redeemer. But the most important resource in my work as a pastor and in our life together as God's people is something we've carried with us every day from the very beginning: the Bible.

What I will call and define as the "biblical narrative" is not only a great read but also what shapes us, forms us, and tells us who we are as beloved people. It is where we must go day after day to remember who we are and what we're called to be about in order that *thy will be done.* The biblical narrative reveals God's purposes for the world, for each of us individually, and for every one of our congregations. How I came to understand the central importance of the gift of this sweeping, grace-filled narrative is the focus of this book.

I have been extraordinarily blessed over the past nine years to serve a congregation that was already on the path to being shaped and empowered by Scripture when I arrived. I cannot fully express how grateful I am to them for opening my eyes to this way of being God's people in the world. We've been through a lot together, and I will be forever in their debt for all they have taught me so far. By God's grace, they'll keep me a little longer. In this book, I refer to them as "Grace Church." I know, and they know, that with a quick Google search you could find out who we really are. But my decision not to call them by their name, I hope, not only displays my respect for them and their ministry but will help the reader see that what we're doing together and how we're moving into God's future is not under our ownership. We are thriving together not because of our own inherent brilliance (although I think there are plenty of incredibly wise folks among them) but because of what God has made us. And I believe—as firmly as I believe in God's constant presence with us—that every single congregation, including yours, may experience joy and a clear sense of our purpose together as you discern alongside one another and in conversation with God what God has created your congregation to be right where you are.

Perhaps best of all, you don't need to purchase an elaborate curriculum or hire an expensive consulting firm. What you do need—and by "you," I mean all of us—is to get serious about your engagement with the biblical narrative. How well do you know it? What stories from it come to mind when you think of what your congregation is currently up to? To what extent are you reaching for this resource when you make decisions about your individual ministry and in your ministry as a congregation?

To head out on this adventure, you'll need to find a translation of the Bible that resonates with you. Maybe a paraphrase would be most helpful or perhaps a Bible with a lot of maps and notes. You really can't go wrong in selecting a Bible *as long as you're reading it with others in your congregation.* If you're reading from a variety of translations, you can look at the similarities and differences, where verses sound beautiful in one translation and where they're jarring in another. The conversations that boil up from this type of engagement with Scripture are invaluable for your life together. Enjoy every minute!

It also might be helpful for you to know, before you begin, that this book arose from a paper I completed in fulfillment of the doctor of ministry in biblical preaching at Luther Seminary in St. Paul, Minnesota. The paper was meant to determine how and to what degree the biblical narrative was allowing Grace Church to thrive in a time of profound and continuing hardship, confusion, and grief. I had a sneaking suspicion that overarching themes and specific stories from the Bible were a significant contributing factor, but what I learned while interviewing the faithful people of Grace Church for the purposes of my paper was astounding. I will include many of the foundational pieces of the interviews during the course of the book but especially in the first chapters. In the latter chapters of the book, the conclusions drawn from the interviews will serve as jumping-off points to explore how one congregation's daily life together was shaped and empowered by Scripture.

My greatest hopes are that this book, and the story of God's work in and through the people of Grace Church, will (1) inspire you to begin to see who you are as *God's beloved people* and (2) drive you to the biblical narrative so that the Holy Spirit may lead you to the discoveries that God needs you to make as you set out to be God's people for the sake of the world.

Those who contributed to the writing of this book are too many to name. Still, a few must be acknowledged. First, thank you to all the people of "Grace Church." You were willing to be vulnerable and share recollections, sometimes very painful memories, in order that God's work in and through your life together would be made known. Thank you for giving me the time to write this manuscript and for supporting me in every facet of my life and ministry. I am humbled to walk alongside you as we serve and love God and our neighbor together.

Thanks to the "Best Cohort Ever" in the DMin program at Luther Seminary. Thank you, Andy, Jeannette, Tracey, Jill, Kenji, Charlie, Rodney, and Susan, for encouraging me in my work as a student and as a pastor and for all you do to serve Jesus Christ where God has placed you.

Thank you to my editor, Beth Gaede at 1517 Media, who read through every draft and never hesitated to say, "Is this the best word choice?"

Thank you to Dr. Kathryn Schifferdecker, who saw something in my DMin project at Luther and encouraged me to share it with a wider readership. Please, never stop writing, teaching, and inspiring preachers.

Finally, thank you to my family: Ken and Eileen—utterly and extraordinarily supportive, loving, and faithful parents who I am proud to call my friends; Amy—beautiful and brilliant sister, artist, writer, and strong woman of faith and my protector from middle school until today; Sam—wise, witty, compassionate, and the most wonderful son I could ever imagine; and Matt—the best pastor I know, the greatest dad on the planet, the kindest man I've met, and by God's grace the life partner I get to walk with every day.

1

WHAT ARE WE DOING HERE, PEOPLE?

What are we doing here, people? It is the question that heralds a breaking point. The line between mild irritation and utter frustration has been crossed. Patience has given way to acute powerlessness. All is not right with the world. "What are we doing here, people?" speaks volumes in our family. Rarely is it directed at anyone in particular. It is a reactive utterance jettisoned into space with no response needed. The one who exclaims it may be moved to these six simple words by any number of exasperating forces, large or small.

Admittedly, it can be a challenge to keep a straight face at times when my partner flings that telling question: we're stuck behind a slow driver, our printer won't leave idle mode, our online banking app repeatedly fails. What causes him to lose all patience is dramatically different from the causes that throw me.

I could contentedly sit at an under-construction intersection all day. When the printer at home refuses to speak kindly to the computer, I go to the library. When the thirtieth attempt to upload the check image on the online banking app fails, I'm happy to head to the credit union.

However, when I burn my favorite brownies that I spent thirty minutes prepping to bake, especially when Godiva chocolate was a casualty, look out. When I mistakenly purchase any article of clothing that requires a delicate wash cycle, keep your head down. And every time I leave my sermon notes at church and have to drive the five whole minutes on a Saturday evening to go get them so I can run through it before bed, anyone in spitting distance will feel it.

Daily irritations aside, this question is also spoken in more serious circumstances. It could erupt after a bad-news prognosis, a broken tooth in December when there's nothing left in the FSA, or another dead-end inpatient program has been reached by a mentally ill loved one.

No matter the situation, this important question reveals, with utter clarity, the role of those in earshot. Now is not the time to offer solutions. If the picture of the check is not uploading in the app, the photographer is not looking for lighting tips. Suggestions about alternate routes to avoid the under-construction intersection would have been useful twenty minutes ago but will definitely not be welcomed now. Similarly, it is decidedly not the time to suggest we should just be grateful we've had money in the FSA at all this year or that our mentally ill loved one has benefitted from so many treatments already that we needn't be greedy. No, when this question is exclaimed, what is most helpful is quiet compassion. And sometimes we get it right.

While no one in my family wants to say or hear the exclamation "What are we doing here, people?" it is actually exceedingly helpful. We've learned, on our best days, to mobilize our forces at its utterance. The time has arrived for listening, offering space, and covering one another with love. On the rare occasion we succeed at holding compassion for one another, layers of trust are constructed and hard anger softens. Life is affirmed, and opportunities for a way forward begin to develop.

Just imagine what the Holy Spirit can do when the church asks this question.

I believe variations on "What are we doing here, people?" are caught in many of our throats in the Christian church today. The church's place in our culture has dramatically shifted. The neighborhoods around us have changed. Worship services that used to require folding chairs to hold the overflow now feel cavernous. The roof leaks in the sanctuary, and the parking lot is falling apart. Our reason for being is, all at once, unclear.

Plenty of us in the church have reached the breaking point, but for all sorts of good reasons, we would rather choke on the all-important question than air it out. We don't want to be negative about the church or to be viewed as unfaithful or lacking trust in God. We don't want to appear like we're giving up, and it would be impossible to accept we can't fix all that seems to have gone wrong. We don't want to risk another heated conversation about worship style or staff configurations. And maybe, we are afraid others will just chalk up our behavior to an alarmist attitude.

What might happen if we threw caution to the wind, the wind of the Holy Spirit, and let that Big Question out?

Over the nine years, I've walked alongside a congregation that had the courage to do just that. By asking the question that had been stuck for so long—"What are we doing here, people?"— the small group of Jesus followers at Grace Church (GC)[1] entered an adventure that continues to shape them. And if anyone had good reasons to stay silent, they had more.

YOU KNOW YOU'RE IN THERE

I promise this book is not intended to invite a competition to determine which church has endured the most or may claim the worst dysfunction. Certainly, we have all endured enough community suffering to participate in such a contest. But that's precisely the point. Below, I present a list of all that the people of GC experienced between the years of 1999 and 2012. I include it because you might find yourself and your congregation somewhere in it. If the cumulative suffering of the wonderful people of GC offers you an opportunity to see some of yourself in the story to come, it will all be worth it:

Accusations of misconduct among the leaders
A charismatic pastor's abrupt departure
Deep grief, division, confusion, and sadness after the departure
Feeling betrayed by the church hierarchy
Feeling lost, without direction
Perceived failure to grow the congregation among the leaders, the youth program, and the congregation as a whole
Dramatic decline in membership
Changes in worship style and time of worship services
Changes in the composition of the neighborhood
Great struggles in communication
A lack of financial resources to support the facilities and the ministries

> Closure of the congregation's preschool
> Anxiety about the very real possibility of closing the
> church[2]

Any one of the above experiences has the potential to sink the ship. Taken together, the list is overwhelming. And overwhelmed the members were. In fact, the words they used to describe their experience of life together at GC throughout this thirteen-year period are unsurprising as well as devastating. Perhaps these words and phrases will sound painfully familiar to you as well: "disappointment, frustration, really upset, uncomfortable, difficult, angst, it exploded, exhausted, frightening, frazzled, discontent, feeling really caught, anxious, shocked, pretty rough, hurt, angry, suffering, time of great difficulty, passionately angry, pretty lethargic, real tense, feeling cranky, antagonistic, not fun, confused, fearful, fall apart, made disruptive, tensions, ended in an explosion, extraordinarily uncomfortable, our fault, too many things to deal with, horrible, insecurity, absurd, in a void, didn't want to deal with it, just unhappy, devastated, lick our wounds, couldn't believe what was happening, went through the roof, shameful, anger and blame, resented, a lot of push back, a nasty time."[3] Alright, so the list *looks* bad. It feels worse. You know it to be true. And when that all-important question "What are we doing here, people?" is not allowed out, these feelings result in destructive behaviors that just compound the hurt.

WHAT DO YOU DO?

So what happens when we, in our churches, don't go for the gusto and ask the Spirit what we're doing here? We still do *something*, and more often than not, it isn't pretty. For just a moment, let's take a closer look at the above words and place them into smaller, very relatable categories.

The first two categories are gimmes: fight and flight.

Trick questions: What happens in a congregation when all sorts of people in it, especially leaders, are exhausted, lethargic, and cranky? What happens when these same struggling leaders are given an overwhelming amount of brokenness to deal with? You guessed it—disconnection. Congregations are filled with people facing all sorts of challenges in their daily lives: addiction, financial stresses, difficulties in primary relationships, chronic pain, and any assortment of other griefs that could lead anyone to despair. How many people have the reserves to invest themselves in even more hurt at church? Running for the hills at a time like this strikes me as a reasonable self-defense tactic.

For others, it's in their blood to go down with the ship. After a number of years of anger, blame, nastiness, and conflict ending in someone going through the roof, only those with the most fight in them can bear it. At this point, congregational meetings end in felony convictions. (If only that were an exaggeration in my denomination.)

Beyond the fight and flight impulses, the people of GC described other responses. To unearth another, let's place a few of the emotions listed above together: fearful, frightened, and confused. Given the very real possibility of closing the church for good, fear and confusion settled in with a number of GC members. Alongside that fear arose a resolve to keep things going at all costs. A type of "not-on-my-watch" attitude gripped them. Whatever it took, these individuals at GC were going to find a way forward. Maybe it would require a staffing change, or shaking up the worship format, or doing whatever was necessary to "get young people" in the building. A group of committed, faithful, and resolute members were not going to go quietly into that dark night.

An analysis of GC's reactions to the great sufferings in their life together would not be complete without one more category. It isn't too difficult to discern what people are thinking when they describe feeling shame about their congregation. A good number of good people at GC felt the diminishing size and vitality of the congregation were their fault. One individual even described feeling embarrassed to be a member of the congregation at gatherings with other local churches. Very few people outside GC knew the specifics, but it was common knowledge around town that things were not going well. Many of us, myself included, would internalize that outside critique. Many came to the understandable but false conclusion that they were to blame.

The categories described above are by no means exhaustive, and the dividing lines between them are easily blurred. Anger and shame often go together. Exhaustion and lethargy can be the unavoidable fallout from assigning blame to others or to oneself. Any combination of the above categories can sink any community in the short or long term. And remaining silent about the emotions and perspectives behind the behaviors only allows the destructive responses to continue.

So what can be done? I believe one question, uttered in the presence of God and by the power of the Holy Spirit, can change everything: "What are we doing here, people?" The people of GC know it firsthand.

THE BIG SHIFT

My account would have great narrative punch if I could tell you one dramatic moment changed everything for GC. If the congregational president, at the annual council retreat, put down her morning coffee and donut and, all of a sudden overcome by the Spirit, shouted, "What are we doing here, people?" that would make for fantastic storytelling. In reality, it took just a little longer. That being said, dramatic change began without complicated policies and procedures or mortgaging the building. In fact, three clear movements set the Spirit loose.

The first unmistakable move was initiated by the pastor. As a pastor, I cannot tell you how ecstatic this makes me. Pastors are human, and far too often, our humanness gets in the way. We get things wrong, we can be quite stubborn, and we have an uncanny ability to make bad situations worse. *And* sometimes, by the grace of God, we get it right! For the people of GC, their pastor (not me!) got it right at just the right moment. Moved by the Spirit in a time of great upheaval, GC's pastor invited the leaders to pray about their life together and ask for the Spirit's guidance. Astounding. It sounds simple, but it goes against every problem-solving impulse so many of us possess. The pastor didn't recommend a Sunday school curriculum, new signage for the property, or adding a staff position. The only life-giving way forward for this congregation was going to have to come from the Spirit as the people of GC listened for God's guidance. The pastor knew it and she said it. Boom.

The second move is at least as important as the first: the leaders did it. They prayed, they listened, and they did it with a posture of surrender. Here, the congregational president was invaluable. Again, as with well-intentioned pastors, congregational leaders are human. They can feel pressure to fix things or right the ship when it's going off course, and particularly in times of desperation, they can lead faith communities in very unhelpful directions. For GC, the congregational president led the way in surrendering to whatever the Spirit revealed. The president, by the power of the Spirit, concluded, "If the congregation dies, it's a part of life. So in the meantime," he asked, "what are we going to do?" Upon reflection on this turn of events, the leader later described what he felt next: "For me that question was a kind of release. It was a kind of faithfulness. And I was confident in God."[4] Did you hear it? "What are we going to do?" was not followed by the need for action. It was followed by a need for and confidence in God. The power of "What are we doing here, people?" was unleashed.

As a result of the first two Spirit-enacted movements, the people of GC were asking The Question. The pastor and the people were beyond mild irritation. They had moved into the territory of utter powerlessness. And for perhaps the first time in years, that place of exasperation did not lead them to disconnection from one another, into angry conflict, into problem-solving mode, or to feelings of embarrassment or shame. With The Question hovering in the air all around them, they did the incredible: they came together.

As I mentioned above, my family has learned that the only helpful, grace-filled response to "What are we doing here, people?" is quiet compassion. It isn't easy. In fact, it goes against every problem-solving impulse we have. But we know from experience that when that level of powerlessness is reached, the time has arrived for listening, offering space to process and decompress, and covering one another with love. On the rare occasion we succeed at holding that space together, layers of trust are constructed, and hard anger softens. Life is affirmed, and opportunities for a way forward begin to develop. The people of GC learned this and lived this. And they went one more Spirit-filled step.

The honest conversations, prayerful reflections, and unstructured time GC held together wherein they were able to listen to

one another and cover one another in love were congregational-
life-altering. Layers of trust were constructed, hard anger was
softened, and life was once again affirmed. The time they set
aside for and with one another did not consist of orchestrated
events complete with soft lighting, burning incense, and great
gospel music, although I don't think any of that would have
hurt. They came together in the one space that would lead them
forward. They came together around the Bible.

The third Spirit-enacted move in the life of GC was their
turn together to the revealing of God's work and will in Genesis through Revelation. Once again, this step was not intended
to solve their problems. They heard the Spirit calling them
together, and a small handful of folks felt the tug to follow that
call through the pages of Scripture. A Bible study led by one lay
leader and a very small group of curious members began slowly
after worship. In fact, that leader who bravely sent out the invitation to this experience was empowered by an "ask" from the
pastor (again, not me). One day she asked if he might pray
about leading a small group Bible study. Yep, that's all it took.
The lay leader had never facilitated a Bible study before, and he
was nervous. He read a great deal to prepare each week and
used many resources to begin engaging with the Bible, everything from Bible commentaries to small group leader guides.
He offered studies from a variety of "canned" curricula at first.
These studies were tremendously helpful to the leader and the
participants because they guided them into encounters with
large biblical concepts like spiritual gifts and types of biblical
literature, such as the parables of Jesus.

Within a couple of years, the leader and a growing number of participants decided they wanted to explore the story of
Jesus in more detail. They couldn't find any curriculum that was
entirely satisfying, so they did something radical. They decided

to read the book of Luke together one verse at a time. They would pause every verse or two for reflection and conversation. No questions were out of bounds, and no one was made to feel inadequate. They found they had more questions than answers, and small group conversations became necessary so everyone could contribute. It took them close to a year to make it all the way through just one Gospel. But their full engagement with God's work and will revealed in the Bible was just beginning.

Without any problem-solving retreats, without a five-year mission plan, without the close watch of trained professionals, the people of GC were coming together. The Spirit was moving among them as they studied and prayed. Life together was shifting. Don't get me wrong; the congregation wasn't flooded with new members and bags full of cash. With their deep dive into Scripture, their problems weren't solved. In fact, more discomfort was right around the corner. But the possibility for new life was tangible. More discoveries were necessary and, unbeknown to them, on the horizon. They would need their newfound confidence in one another because what they discovered, where Bible study led them, would push any community to the brink.

2

WHY ARE WE DYING HERE, PEOPLE?

With the three movements of the Spirit in full swing, new life, new beginnings, and new opportunities to experience fullness of life in Jesus Christ were everywhere. Grace Church (GC) welcomed their new pastor, and they were getting along swimmingly. The great start could be attributed, in part, to the tremendous work the congregation did in the interim period before she arrived. They had countless cottage meetings to receive input. Those who couldn't make the meetings were contacted directly, so every member had the opportunity to contribute their two cents. Prayers were ascending constantly that God would guide the process and that the congregation would follow God's leading. By the power of the Holy Spirit, the call became clear, and the daily work between the new pastor and the congregation—developing relationships, discovering one another's priorities, figuring out where the light switches are in the sanctuary, and the like—began as they walked alongside one another in faith.

This partnership was also bound to flourish because the congregation had been so clear about their expectations for the new pastor. She received a list, day one, of the priorities of the congregation as they discerned God's purposes for them. At the top of the list was a dream the congregation had held for quite some time: to build a bridge with the preschool.

GC had opened a preschool almost sixty years prior to the new pastor's arrival. It began because, at that time, the state was not offering kindergarten for all children, and the congregation felt passionately about providing access to education for the young children in their community. Over the years, they welcomed hundreds of families and were exceedingly grateful to accompany them on their educational journey. The pastor led weekly chapel worship for the preschool for decades, and the congregation felt they were answering God's call to serve through this vibrant ministry.

Their commitment to this preschool ministry only grew as the relationship between the congregation and the preschool became strained. One former pastor, years before, had mentioned to the leaders that they felt the preschool was the best thing the congregation had going. For some, the sting of that assessment remained just under the surface. In the years leading up to the new pastor's arrival, however, difficulties arose, as difficulties do, and it became clear that the preschool director was unhappy. Enter the new pastor. Yep, that's me.

Hearing the congregation's determination to repair their relationship with the preschool director and leaders, I got going. I wrote thank-you notes. I showed up at staff meetings to celebrate the wonderful work of the teachers and assisting staff. I made myself available any time to the director and the congregational president, and both individuals committed to making a fresh start.

Great things started to happen. The committed and faithful preschool board was charged up about their work, I connected with the parents and kids, and before long, a few families were visiting worship. People felt welcomed and loved by the GC congregation when we held teacher appreciation lunches and gave gifts. I was new to this whole preschool and church relationship, so I invited a consultant to come and help our congregational leaders connect more deeply with the preschool teachers and staff. We were firing on all cylinders, and the future looked bright. That is, until May rolled around and the director submitted her letter of resignation.

Confusion is too weak a word for the way I, and the church leaders, felt. Was I too eager in my leadership? Absolutely. Did I make mistakes because of my lack of experience with preschool ministry? Without a doubt. But I thought we were communicating well and had each other's back. And it was going to get worse—much worse.

One by one, the teachers informed me that they too were leaving. I admit, I started to panic. The church leaders were handling each blow with kindness and the nonanxious presence to which *I* was called, but I was reeling. How could this happen? We worked so hard! Sadness, frustration, and a growing sense of the real possibility that we would not be able to put a staff together for the following fall began to take hold.

The GC leaders did what they had done consistently throughout my less than twelve months with them. They rose to the occasion. They organized a beautiful farewell and appreciation event for the preschool director and offered gifts and gratitude for the departing teachers. The preschool board called meetings to pray for God's guidance and drafted position descriptions for immediate posting. We waited for God to provide.

After about a month, now well into the summer, we hadn't received a single qualified applicant. Parents of our preschoolers wondered, rightfully so, what our plan was for the coming academic year. I had no idea what to do. The preschool board asked me to draft two letters—one that asked the preschool families for patience as we continued our search and one that announced the closure of the school. The preschool board and the congregational council set a date for a meeting to determine what course of action we would take.

I cannot express fully how devastated I was by this turn of events. This congregation had asked me to "build a bridge with the preschool," and in less than a year, I was the pastor on duty when this ministry of six decades might end. That "not-on-my-watch" feeling? I had it in spades.

I'll never forget that decision-point meeting. Around the tables in our primary preschool classroom sat all of the council and preschool board members I had grown to love and respect. Each member was given the opportunity to give, prayerfully and faithfully, their opinion about how to proceed. With no new qualified applicants for the position of director and no way to offer the quality preschool education to which the church was committed, the choice was clear: close it. It was on my watch that the preschool closed. These wonderful people had been through so much already, and now this vibrant, service-centered ministry closed up shop.

I couldn't wrap my head around what had just taken place. Before I arrived and in my first months as pastor, the congregation had just begun to recognize the powerful movement of the Holy Spirit among them. It had taken a number of years and more hurt than anyone thought possible to develop that awareness, but GC had received a glimpse of newness of life in Jesus Christ. Hallelujah! Was it a gift? Yes! A miracle? Most definitely! But was it the new beginning that launched GC into an upward trajectory for years to come? Not a chance.

The glorious, God-given energy and hope that the people of GC had received in the previous couple of years were absolutely what they needed. They needed that hope to help them heal from all that came before. *And they received that hope to fortify them for what was to come.* It didn't take long before the people of GC began to experience a truth in the form of a pattern in their life together: *there is no resurrection without death.*

This discovery seems like a no-brainer. We do, after all, follow a *crucified* Lord: "Then [Jesus] began to teach them that the Son of Man must undergo great suffering, and be rejected by the elders, the chief priests, and the scribes, and be killed, and after three days rise again" (Mark 8:31). In my faith tradition, we describe baptism as a daily dying and rising—a dying to the old self and a rising as a new creation by the power of God in Christ each and every day. As the apostle Paul declares, "For if we have been united with him in a death like his, we will certainly be united with him in a resurrection like his" (Rom 6:5). More than that, however, Jesus's own words describe this reality over and over again:

> Very truly, I tell you, unless a grain of wheat falls into the earth and dies, it remains just a single grain; but if it dies, it bears much fruit. (John 12:24)

> For those who want to save their life will lose it, and those who lose their life for my sake, and for the sake of the gospel, will save it. (Mark 8:35)

"Very truly, I tell you, when you were younger, you used to fasten your own belt and to go wherever you wished. But when you grow old, you will stretch out your hands, and someone else will fasten a belt around you and take you where you do not wish to go." (He said this to indicate the kind of death by which he would glorify God.) After this he said to him, "Follow me." (John 21:18–19)

Jesus tries to tell his disciples—then and now—how life in Christ, by the leading of the Holy Spirit, works. Resurrection is what God is all about. *And* the new life of resurrection always and only follows the death of what was.

So I'll just say it: I don't like it! I don't enjoy death. I don't desire it. I don't seek it out. But as we follow our crucified and risen Lord on the path *God* sets before us, death comes to us. It hurts. It's painful. Grief rises up. Anger swells. In all honesty, I'd rather not go through that, thank you very much. Yet the truth remains. Whether I like it or not, death is a necessary part of faithful living. As the people of GC and I learned together, it happens over and over again.

The people of GC were well acquainted with death long before I arrived. They had walked past the vacant small chairs in Sunday school classrooms for years. They had felt the effects of many a community project failing to produce new members. They had watched beautiful stained glass windows fall into rotted window frames and the organ pipes lean in on one another without the personnel or a dime to fix any of it. Now the beloved preschool was a memory. It hurt. It all hurt. Even as new life was sprouting, the real-life experience of death didn't go away. It didn't magically disappear. And as the GC congregation's trust in one another deepened, they opened the door to reveal some of that pain. They didn't really know what to do with that pain. But as they gathered around the gift of the Bible, the Spirit revealed a shocking response God's people had offered throughout the millennia: lament.

LAMENT, THE BIBLE, AND US

I grew up in a midwestern family that was very loving. My parents are extraordinarily supportive, affirming, and faithful people. They let me know every day that I was loved and valued. And even in this loving, nurturing environment, I was all too familiar with the phrase "walk it off." Fall down and scrape a knee? Walk it off. Get humiliated in a softball game? Walk it off. Completely tank zoology? Walk it off. This advice is remarkably helpful in many situations. Who really wants to be a blubbering mess in front of their zoology professor? I daresay I've unearthed this advice from my parenting toolbox more than once.

But contrary to the wisdom of many midwesterners like myself, "walk it off" is not a commandment. In fact, the people of God in our most holy book of books show us a dramatically different way:

How long, O Lord? Will you forget me forever?
How long will you hide your face from me?
How long must I bear pain in my soul,
and have sorrow in my heart all day long?
How long shall my enemy be exalted over me? (Ps 13:1–2)

O God, you have rejected us, broken our defenses;
you have been angry; now restore us!
You have caused the land to quake; you have torn it open;
repair the cracks in it, for it is tottering.

19

You have made your people suffer hard things;
> you have given us wine to drink that made us reel.
>> (Ps 60:1–3)

This is language poured out from mascara-running, nose-dripping grief, spoken from lips contorted with weeping. These are spit-soaked words uttered as a fist is shaken at the heavens. This is honesty without reservation, grief laid bare, unflinching sadness and anger. And here's the million-dollar question: Can you imagine saying any of this in polite company?

Not only are these words jarring because of the raw emotions expressed in them, but to some of us, they sound downright blasphemous. Did you notice that the psalmists are not raging against the world in general, flinging their angry tirades at anyone who might listen? They blame God (gasp!). More than that, they *tell* God that God is to blame. In fact, in so many passages of lament, God and no one else is blamed for the people's suffering. In Psalm 60 alone, the people raise their voices repeatedly in a brazen accusation of God: *You* have rejected! *You* have caused! *You* have made your people suffer! But it gets worse.

Perhaps the most pointed lament speech against God in the entire biblical witness comes to us from the prophet Habakkuk. Habakkuk sees violence all around and *demands* a response from God:

O Lord, how long shall I cry for help,
> and you will not listen?
Or cry to you "Violence!"
> and you will not save?
Why do you make me see wrongdoing
> and look at trouble?

Destruction and violence are before me;
    strife and contention arise.
So the law becomes slack
    and justice never prevails.
The wicked surround the righteous—
    therefore judgment comes forth perverted.
      (Hab 1:2–4)

Habakkuk accuses God not only of allowing injustice to prevail but of making him witness it. With all of the bluster of a child stubbornly testing a parent, Habakkuk rails against God, "I will stand at my watchpost, and station myself on the rampart; I will keep watch to see what he will say to me, and what he will answer concerning my complaint" (Hab 2:1). These accusatory, grief-laden words are included in our most holy book. And if you're feeling uncomfortable with it, you are not alone.

Discomfort with and outright rejection of pointed lament have a long history among God's people. Faithful God followers from many generations have asked, Could such language ever be appropriate in our relationship with God? We are created beings. Isn't it a gross overstepping of our creatureliness to accuse God in this way? We need look no further than the midrash (interpretations of Scripture from the Jewish community in centuries past) of Habakkuk to find companions in our shock at these words. One scholar, upon investigating the volumes of midrash, can't help but name-call: "The Midrash deems Habakkuk guilty of speaking rashly before God, emulating an ignoramus rather than a prophet."[1]

Yet if we're honest, how many faithful people from generation to generation feel the way Habakkuk and the psalmists did? Have *you* ever felt frustrated, helpless, angry, or abandoned by God's seeming inaction in the face of your suffering or the suffering of others? Have you ever wanted to call God out but stopped short? If you have, I'm right there with you. And we are joined by faithful people throughout the centuries who have held their tongues. But to what end? If we do not direct our grief and anger at God, we know those feelings will work themselves out in other ways. We've experienced it together as we lash out at one another and as individuals as we grow evermore withdrawn into our own sense of powerlessness. We may feel that to let our lament soar is to endanger our relationship with one another or with God. But quite the opposite is true. In fact, lament is a unique kind of faithfulness.

GOD CAN TAKE IT, AND SO MUST WE

What remains so fascinating about lament throughout the Bible is that God's response in the face of honest lament is not at all what we would expect. Drawing on imagery from our popular culture, I might expect the heavens to open and a bolt of lightning to consume Habakkuk in flames. Or God could show up like a contemporary antihero, fed up with an ungrateful creation, and take us all out with guns blazing. But unrestrained divine smiting just isn't God's way with God's people, especially in times of lament. I suspect it has something to do with the faithfulness of the act of lament itself.

While lament has been rejected as unfaithful by current and previous generations, for God's people to raise their voices in lament is, finally, *an act of faith that God has power to do something about suffering.* God's people cry out to God in lament because we ultimately trust that creation and all that is in it endure because God has "pledged in an eternal covenant that it shall endure."[2] Lament is the cry of a people who know that their hope may be found only in God's steadfast love and faithfulness. Lament is the cry of a people who know that the only future for the church is the one God envisions and the one God enacts. The survival of God's people—whether as individuals, communities, or institutions—rests completely on God's initiative. Who God's people are and who they will be are determined by God alone. Whatever we are and whatever we will be are in the hands of our God.

Now we arrive where we began, in the hands of the crucified God.

What are we doing here, people? We are following the God who was killed for the life of the world. As we follow faithfully, death is a necessary piece of the experience. Grief is unavoidable. So we'd better start talking about it.

Lamenting together certainly wasn't a part of the plan for the people of GC. But soon, the work they had done in opening up to one another about their relationship with God through Bible study became the foundation upon which they were able to be vulnerable with one another in shared lament. They began to give voice to painful stories from their life together: "Do you remember the so-and-so family? I wonder what happened to them. I miss them." "We tried to make that ministry work, didn't we? We worked so hard at it. We were doing what we thought God wanted us to do. Why did it do so much damage in the end?" "That council meeting was awful. We just didn't know what to do." Honest grief, sadness, and frustration—in the form of lament—were let out in the open, where they could be offered to the God whose steadfast love and faithfulness know no limits.

As you may expect, anxieties would arise among the congregation of GC when these situations were dug up from the pit, but anxiety wouldn't overcome these bold Jesus followers.

Because they had entered into a deeper relationship with one another *through Scripture*, their sharing had a grace-filled quality to it. In all of these situations, when past and present hurts surfaced among them, they didn't take the usual route, the path of least resistance. They didn't revert back to their old patterns of withdrawal, blame, or vitriol. Now their hurt was met with compassionate nods and an appreciation of each other's frustration. Standing alongside one another as a people of death and resurrection, they dared to accept what could not be explained or reasoned through.

They began to see how their losses weren't unique or reason for shame. Time spent dwelling in the Bible led them to stories of loss after loss, end after end, death after death. They were beginning to understand their losses in the context of the losses of God's people from generation to generation. Hannah's grief over her inability to have children, Joseph's anger at the betrayal of his brothers, and Jeremiah's grand lament over his role as a rejected prophet all took on new meaning for the people of GC.

Their shared experience of loss, of goodbyes and endings, of death itself was no longer a taboo subject. The feelings of anger, grief, fear, and frustration around those experiences of death no longer threatened to weaken the community. In fact, they brought them together even more. As they gave voice to their lament in the face of death, they experienced the shared reality of God's people from generation to generation. They allowed their questions to remain. And with questions left out in the open, they could finally hear the response *from the One who was able to show the way forward.*

3

WHERE DO WE GO
FROM HERE, PEOPLE?

Messy tears, powerlessness laid bare, nerve endings exposed—welcome to the ministry of Grace Church (GC)! Not exactly the mission statement we were hoping to share. The congregation had been through so much, and now they were deep in it again—no answers, lots of grief, completely in the dark as to what would happen next. This isn't what the people had in mind when they welcomed their new pastor. Admittedly, it wasn't what I had in mind either. I wonder if that was part of the problem.

Near the end of Luke's Gospel, after Jesus's resurrection, we're given a story that has power for just this kind of moment, where all of our hope-filled expectations disappoint us. A couple of guys are on the road walking away from Jerusalem, on their way to a town called Emmaus. They're stunned at what has taken place. A man, Jesus, who they believed would change the world, alter history, get things back on the rails for their people, was just crucified. Some stranger shows up in their midst and expresses interest in their conversation. The stranger sounds clueless about the events that are consuming their thoughts. They give the down-and-dirty summary and complete their story with this mournful declaration: "But we had hoped that he was the one to redeem Israel" (Luke 24:21). Hear that? *But we had hoped.* I dare you not to feel their disappointment and anger-tinged sadness. God bless them for their honesty. "But we had hoped God had actually done what God promised." How long, O Lord?

In much the same way, the people of GC had their hopes disappointed. We had hoped that together, we'd put the past struggles behind us. We had hoped we would have celebration after celebration. We had hoped death was in the rearview mirror and that the "fullness of life" thing that Jesus talked about would define us. At least, that's what I was thinking.

Each week, I'd look at the worship numbers and the budget numbers to see if we were "successful" or not. GC called a new pastor to help them turn things around, to get things in the black, to build bridges. At least, that was what I thought. How many of us as congregational members and leaders believe that a successful ministry is one that involves gain and growth? I wouldn't necessarily have admitted it at the time, but you bet I believed it. But the gain and growth model of ministry has everything to do with human desires and expectations, not with the way God so often chooses to work in the world.

To say it is difficult to stare death in the face is a dramatic understatement and an insult to those going through it. The pain, anger, confusion, and deep sadness that accompany death are often beyond words. It is a devastating truth that to be about the ministry of Jesus Christ is to follow him to and through death. We are God's people, called to face our own brokenness and the brokenness around us. We walk through our own valleys of the shadow of death, and we accompany others through theirs. The biblical witness reveals this again and again. Hannah's suffering and despair were not storytelling devices. The Psalms were not written in response to hypothetical experiences. Jesus's death has real-life implications for us. Jesus's "success" was not measured by increased worship numbers and budgets in the black. He followed God's will for the life of the world wherever God showed the way, and the way God revealed was through the cross. This is the ministry to which we are called. There is no bypass around death to resurrection.

The people of GC knew this and lived it. They faced it and bore it. But even more than that, they shared it. They dug into their Bibles and shared their stories. They came together in honesty and in grief. Now they would become acquainted with the way God responds in the face of death, the same way God has been responding for millennia.

MORE TO THE STORY

Did I mention my gigantic failure with regard to the preschool was the worst beginning of a vacation ever?

The morning after The Vote to close the preschool, I hopped on a plane with my family for a trip back to the Midwest, the first vacation our family had planned after I began as GC's pastor. I felt as if a dark cloud hovered over me. The sun shone all around me, on everyone and everything else, but I couldn't feel it. I had let these incredible people down. They had trusted me to lead, and I led them to catastrophic failure. To make matters worse, no one was mad at me. No one took their grief or sadness out on me. I could have taken some solace in defending myself and my actions if anyone in the congregation had come after me. But they were kind and affirming and had figured out that we were in this together, come what may. I had some serious catching up to do.

After a few days of separation from The Vote, I relaxed a bit. My congregational president even called once to make sure I was all right. This wasn't their first rodeo, and they were praying for God to point the way. I wasn't there yet. I was licking my wounds and, truth be told, nursing my maimed ego, my recognition that I wasn't the "successful" pastor I knew they deserved. Then I got the call.

On a soggy midwestern afternoon, my cell phone rang. It was a cold call from a new nonprofit that had opened just down the street from GC. They were looking for a location. New to the city, the organization had only a small office, and they would need classrooms for the recently arrived refugees they had just begun helping learn English, complete immigration paperwork, and write résumés. The kind woman on the other line asked, "You wouldn't happen to have any classroom space available, would you?" I had to sit down. The congregation was praying for God's direction, but could it really arrive this quickly and in such obvious fashion? So many questions crossed my mind that I forgot to respond. After a few seconds of silence, she asked if I was still there. "Yes, yes!" I nearly yelled. "I think this might be a Holy Spirit thing!" I remember this response because, after saying it, I realized it didn't sound overly eloquent or pastor-like. I sounded desperate, which, of course, I was.

After getting the woman's information and collecting myself enough for a somewhat less giddy goodbye, I began to dial the number for my congregational president. I hesitated. Would she be as excited? Was I going too quickly? Was there something wrong with this picture that I wasn't seeing? Would I be leading my folks down another path of grief and disappointment? I was more than a little unsure of myself and my leadership.

If I thought about her request any longer, I knew I'd talk myself out of it, so I decided to risk another embarrassing ministry debacle and dialed. Moments after sharing the news, GC's fearless president took action. She called a meeting of the leaders. They scheduled an information session with the new nonprofit. And as they say, the rest is history. I didn't lead the congregation astray because the congregation was praying even harder than I. They had walked through the valley together once again. They had named their grief and sadness. They were ready for what God would do next. They were ready for resurrection.

We've been together nearly nine years now, this young nonprofit and GC, and the partnership between our ministries is a significant piece of who we both are. The people of GC poured their gifts for hospitality, education, and justice seeking and their love for children into this new partnership. The newly arrived refugees shared their openness, courage, tenacity, resourcefulness, and unshakable faith. Was it all smooth sailing? Not by a long shot. Plumbing emergencies, property damage, and volumes of miscommunication would follow. But God was present and active. The Spirit was creating something brand new. None of us knew where it was going; we still don't, but God's work of resurrection is all over it. Who knew God was in the business of resurrection? Oh, right, every New Testament writer and much of the Old Testament witness. There's that.

GOD HAS SOMETHING TO SAY ABOUT THAT

As it turns out, the witness of Scripture, throughout both the Old and New Testaments, is that God is the God of resurrection and life. God finds a way. Or, more accurately, God *makes* a way. Psalm 30 comes to mind:

> O Lord, you brought up my soul from Sheol,
> > restored me to life from among those gone down to
> > the Pit. (30:3)

> You have turned my mourning into dancing;
> > you have taken off my sackcloth
> > and clothed me with joy. (30:11)

Because God is the God of resurrection and life, even in the deepest valley as cries of lament fill our mouths, we are given gifts to shore us up and sustain us for all that is to come. Sound too good to be true? I agree! Good thing we have the Bible.

Throughout Scripture, what follows on the heels of lament is downright shocking. When death arrives, when dead ends prevent God's people from finding a way forward, when grief and sadness begin to swallow up our ancestors, God moves in astounding ways. God's responses include but are not limited to assurances of God's presence, God's promise to provide, and God's intention and action to bring about new beginnings. But as if that's not enough, God responds to the people with God's gift of *identity*. *God tells the people who they are.* As despair nips at the heels of God's people, God shows up over and over to remind them who they are as beloved receivers of God's faithfulness and newness of life.

To get us started, let's catch up with God's people at one of their lowest moments: the exile. The people of God have been delivered by God from oppression in Egypt. God has led them through the wilderness to the land of promise, the land flowing with milk and honey. Once in the land, no foreign power reigns over them. The great king David expands their territory. David's son, Solomon, constructs the Lord's temple in the middle of the Holy City of Jerusalem. Prosperity and order seem to signal the blessing of God that will never end. But when Solomon dies, the brokenness of the people's rulers and the people themselves, always present just beneath the surface, boils over. Oppressive rulers, greed, and injustice gain the upper hand. God's people, and the land God has given them, are divided. The people's trust, instead of being placed in the hands of a loving God, is given over to alliances with foreign powers. Before long, the catastrophe they never believed possible unfolds before them. God's people are hauled away from the land, their leaders in chains, and the Holy City of Jerusalem is razed to the ground.

Cries of anguish flood God's ears. God's chosen people have been unfaithful. What will God do now? God would be justified in leaving them to their own plans, their own devices. But God does not ignore the despair of the people. God will not forget them. No, God does something else entirely, something so filled with grace that it's almost unbelievable. God's word comes to the people in exile, in profound grief, and declares,

> But now thus says the Lord,
> > he who created you, O Jacob,
> > he who formed you, O Israel:
> Do not fear, for I have redeemed you;
> > I have called you by name, you are mine.
> When you pass through the waters, I will be with you;
> > and through the rivers, they shall not overwhelm you;
> when you walk through fire you shall not be burned,
> > and the flame shall not consume you.
> For I am the Lord your God,
> > the Holy One of Israel, your Savior.

I give Egypt as your ransom,
>   Ethiopia and Seba in exchange for you.
Because you are precious in my sight,
>   and honored, and I love you,
I give people in return for you,
>   nations in exchange for your life.
Do not fear, for I am with you;
>   I will bring your offspring from the east,
>   and from the west I will gather you;
I will say to the north, "Give them up,"
>   and to the south, "Do not withhold;
bring my sons from far away
>   and my daughters from the end of the earth—
everyone who is called by my name,
>   whom I created for my glory,
>   whom I formed and made." (Isa 43:1–7)

The people know they have betrayed the Lord their God. They know the grief they have caused their Lord, their Creator, their Sustainer, their Deliverer. And now, God responds to their rejection and betrayal by pronouncing them *already* redeemed. God calls them by name and claims them in intimate relationship. They will not be consumed by fire or overwhelmed by raging rivers. God's promise for newness of life is already being enacted with the reassurance that in the future God will gather the people again. A new reality breaks into their overwhelming grief: hope. Even as the people continue to endure separation from one another and from the land, hope is a *current* possibility because God has decided to be present with the people and carry them through whatever may threaten them. Hope is also a *future* possibility as God promises to gather the people again, to "bring [God's] sons from far away and

[God's] daughters from the end of the earth" (Isa 43:6). But wait! There's more . . .

We hear this message of God's grace and the gift of hope again on the lips of Jesus in John 17. The context is dramatically different, but the experience of grief, fear, and sadness on the part of God's people is the same. In a passage from what is known as Jesus's farewell discourse in John's Gospel, Jesus seeks to reassure his followers. They've had a pretty rough night. On the night Jesus was betrayed, they receive the news that Judas, one of their own, will betray Jesus. Then Jesus informs them that Peter will deny him before the cock crows. Next, they hear the time has come for Jesus to leave them, and where he is going, they cannot follow. As if that weren't enough, Jesus drops all sorts of other painful information: "They will put you out of the synagogues. Indeed, an hour is coming when those who kill you will think that by doing so they are offering worship to God" (John 16:2). I've had some rough nights, but nothing that comes close to that. Jesus's beloved friends are undoubtedly scared, not knowing what will come next. Into this fear-filled, grieving group, Jesus offers a prayer to the Father they are intended to overhear: "All mine are yours, and yours are mine; and I have been glorified in them. . . . Holy Father, protect them in your name that you have given me, so that they may be one, as we are one. . . . Righteous Father, the world does not know you, but I know you; and these know that you have sent me. I made your name known to them, and I will make it known, so that the love with which you have loved me may be in them, and I in them" (John 17:10, 11b, 25–26).

Jesus tells them, come what may, they are one with the Father and the Son. He tells these constant companions they have been handpicked by the Father and the Father will protect them. These struggling Jesus followers are not abandoned. They will not be left alone. Once again, hope is a current and future possibility because of what God has done, is doing, and will do for them. God has taken the initiative to call them, sustain them, and now reassure them that the love God has for the Son is the love that will live in them.

The gift of hope is powerful. It is life giving. Yet in these passages, and so many others just like them in our Most Holy Book of Books, hope is just the beginning. What God chooses to give next is a game changer. God's love and grace overcome despair, hallelujah! Now from this place of hope and promise, God has one more beautiful move to make with and for us. With that hope alive and at work in us, God finally tells us who we are.

Allow me one detour from Isaiah and John to pick up an image from the Prophets that provides us with everything we need to know. The prophet Ezekiel stands in a valley of dry bones. He sees what has become of God's people: they are lifeless, destitute, with nothing left. But then, with all the grace God can throw at them, the bones are revived. They are revived by the breath of God through God's very Spirit. To me, that's hope. They have connective tissue and all they need to exist. God says, "I will lay sinews on you, and will cause flesh to come upon you, and cover you with skin, and put breath in you, and you shall live" (Ezek 37:6). But God wasn't satisfied with bodies that were simply breathing. When Ezekiel obeyed the command of the Lord to prophesy to those breath-filled bodies, they did one more thing: "The breath came into them, and they lived, and stood on their feet" (37:10b). Is breathing a good thing? Yes. Necessary? Yes. But what an extraordinary feeling to stand on your own two feet! That's the gift that follows hope. With hope you can breathe again, feel your connective tissue pulling you back together. But to stand up straight on your own two feet again is to have a posture of confidence, a posture of preparedness for whatever might come next. And by the grace of God, we are empowered to stand on our own two feet, confident in who God made us and what God might have in store for us, when we know *who we are*. We hold on to hope not as an end point but as a beginning. Hope is what allows us to see the sun after the rain. But it is identity, who we are as God's beloved children, that places us on the Spirit's starting blocks. The breath of hope was given to those dry bones, and they were restored as whole bodies once again. But when they stood on their own two feet ready to move where God called, they were Israel, God's beloved and chosen people.

In John's Gospel and in the book of Isaiah, the people are given the hope that God is working on them and around them. Jesus's stunned followers and the exiled people of God receive a renewed promise to grasp with both hands. But God wills even more for them. God—right in the midst of their struggles, fears, confusion, and chaos—reaffirms their identity, *who they are as God's people.*

The people have been created for the Lord's glory. They are a people who have been chosen, formed, and made by God. The Lord declares, "You are precious in my sight, and honored, and I love you" (Isa 43:4). Jesus proclaims the love with which the Father loved *him* will be in *them*. They may be *one* with one another as they are *one* with Jesus and the Father. They are loved, honored, and precious to God, whatever their present circumstances. Therefore, they are invited to live! *As God's beloved children, they may now anticipate being gathered with all God's beloved in God's future.* This has tremendous ramifications for daily living. Their God has not been defeated. They need not be resigned to the triumph of death. Jesus's death will not be the final word. God's works of restoration, renewal, and love are present and imminent. Daily life is now infused with such a sense of God's presence and ultimate will that God's people may *live accordingly*. Fear, anxiety, grief, scarcity, abandonment, and lack of identity are no longer the people's defining reality in exile or the disciples' defining reality at Christ's crucifixion and ascension. God has made a new way available for them. God has called them to a life of hope, promise, and trust *even as they are still facing their immediate, grueling, and nearly incomprehensible circumstances.*

Now, lest you imagine the passages from Isaiah and John are extraordinary in the context of the biblical witness, remember this: God's work for resurrection, new life, and renewal in our identity as God's beloved children is everywhere! Our Bibles are filled with such instances: Hosea 14:4–7; Jeremiah 29:11–14; Matthew 28:16–20; Acts 2:1; and more. In all of these situations, God's people are in the thick of it. They are struggling through what appear to be insurmountable, dead-end conditions. Yet God's word of hope and the call to be God's beloved people in the world come again and again. God takes the initiative. God provides the breath of life. And God tells the people who they are as God's beloved so they may stand on their own two feet once again.

MEANWHILE, BACK AT THE RANCH

The people of GC have endured one death valley after the next. Closing their preschool was one of the first I experienced with them, and it certainly wouldn't be the last. Honest lament and opportunities to voice our grief have been and continue to be essential elements of our life together. It was our shared grief, and the brave expression of it, that brought God's people together millennia ago. It has the power to hold us together today. We cry out to the Lord because it is the Lord who has the ability to do something about the suffering we experience. And when we join our grief-filled voices with those of God's people throughout the generations, we then stand alongside them to hear God's response.

Make no mistake; the congregation of GC needed and continues to need God's hope every single day. Even when we're firing on all cylinders, death is always just one moment away. We need God's breath to enliven us and strengthen us with grace-filled connective tissue. But we also need God to set us on our own two feet. *We need God's word to remind us who we are.* This is the story that is told over and over again in the Bible, the story into which God calls us and for which God equips us: God gathers us and sends us into the world in order that we may be God's beloved people. This is who we are, and this is our purpose day in and day out.

But please, don't just take my word for it. Much more has been said and needs to be said about the hope and central identity we receive as the Holy Spirit guides us in our encounter with the biblical narrative. Dare to join me for a deeper dive? Brush off your academic reading glasses; we're going in!

4

WHO ARE WE
HERE, PEOPLE?

Time to come clean. I've been holding something important back, and it's time to get it out in the open: I have a bias. Like all biases, it's controversial. Some theological giants and biblical scholars vehemently disagree with me, but not all do. It's a bias that has grown over the years and through my interaction with the people of Grace Church (GC) has become downright foundational for my understanding of the totality of the biblical witness. You certainly do not have to agree with me, but I challenge you to consider it seriously before you decide if it has teeth or, as my grandmother would say, it's a bunch of hooey.

What's my bias? Here goes. The Bible, from Genesis to Revelation, has one dominant narrative: The pervasive action of God, throughout Scripture, is to create life and to bring individuals and peoples through death to resurrection. In God's persistent, steadfast love and faithfulness, God creates life where there is no life and works resurrection among the dead. Full stop. How did I arrive at that definition? Here's the short version:

In the Old Testament, throughout God's glorious interaction with creation, we experience God's initiative to create life where there is no life. God creates all things from the seas of chaos and establishes covenants with Noah and Abram. God creates a people by leading the Israelites from oppression in Egypt through the wilderness to the land of promise. God reveals God's love and faithfulness to the people even as they are exiled from the land, promising to bring about new life. Within these larger events, God provides Hannah with a son and Ezekiel with a vision of dry bones receiving the breath of life, and the Old Testament is brought to a close with the promise that God will send Elijah to "turn the hearts of parents to their children and the hearts of children to their parents, so that [God] will not come and strike the land with a curse" (Mal 4:6).

God's unrelenting work for life continues throughout the New Testament witness. Elizabeth has a son in her old age. Mary, who had not known a man, carries the Son of God. The Son's life and ministry are marked by constant acts of healing and restoration. Jesus lifts up the lowly and fills the hungry with good things. The full force of human brutality and disregard for the gift of life are violently visited on God's Son. But excruciating suffering and death do not prevail. God is not to be held in a tomb. God's will for life is stronger than the oppression of an empire, and God will not be stopped. As the risen Christ ascends, new life runs rampant in the giving of the Spirit. Saul's persecutions and Peter's narrow vision are no match for God's insistence upon life. Even as the destructive forces of empire continue their seemingly unstoppable march, the vision of God's heavenly throne room and God's promise to make all things new are the final grace-filled revelations of this biblical narrative.

In my faith tradition, it would only be right for you to take my biased, controversial assertion and debate it over a cup of coffee or an adult beverage. Please do! Just be aware that in this bias rests my confession and testimony. I will not change it quickly or easily. I am also slow to revise it because I have seen it in action as this narrative has captured the Spirit-enlightened imagination of the people of GC. This is the narrative that has provided comfort, hope, and healing to GC. But more than anything else, *this is the biblical narrative that has shaped their identity.*

What are the people of God at GC doing here? They are living out their identity as a people gathered in the name of Jesus Christ, empowered by the Holy Spirit, and called God's beloved children. What does that mean? They are a priestly kingdom and a holy nation. They are those whom God has handed over to Jesus that they may be one with God the Father and the Lord Jesus Christ. They are the people with whom God in Christ abides. They are a scattered remnant that was not forsaken by God but gathered together by the Spirit. They are who God, through the biblical narrative, says they are—called to live out their identity as God's beloved children, created, sustained, and made new over and over again for the sake of the world. (We'll get to that last "for the sake of the world" part in a moment.)

A PHILOSOPHER AND THEOLOGIAN BLOWS OUR MINDS

If the above assertion that the biblical narrative shapes our identity as God's beloved children has blown your righteous mind (as it has blown mine), I want to be certain that you know I didn't make it up. I'd love to take credit for it, but I can't. This bold argument originated in minds far superior to mine. In fact, this basic conclusion—that narrative shapes our identity—has broad acceptance in the world of academia. Rolf Jacobson, professor of Old Testament at Luther Seminary, says it best: "In recent years, philosophers, cognitive psychologists, theologians, anthropologists and sociologists . . . have actually arrived at a shocking thing: consensus. And the consensus is that the warp and woof of human identity is narrative."[1]

Still, one philosopher in particular has inspired many a child of God on this path of discovery. His name is Paul Ricœur. I offer you an oversimplified yet still painfully academic summary of his argument in the hope that it will provide you with not only a foundation for my arguments that follow but a way to begin to reflect on what narrative may be shaping your sense of identity. (Caveat: If at any time you are frustrated, bored, or otherwise put off by this academic summary, please do not hesitate to jump ahead. Understanding Ricœur's philosophy is not essential reading for all that is to come.)

French philosopher and theologian Paul Ricœur, in his three-volume work, *Time and Narrative*, establishes the formative role of narrative in the development of identity—specifically an identity of the self within time.[2] For the purposes of this book, two major topics are of importance: Ricœur's work with Aristotle's forms of emplotment and with the concept of threefold mimesis.

Ricœur borrows from the work of Aristotle's *Poetics* to establish the role of *emplotment* in forming the self. Simply defined, emplotment is "the organization of events."[3] The events we select from our lives and how we organize them inform how we understand our identity, our sense of self. The self operates in what

Aristotle refers to as the threefold present, "the dialectic of expectation, memory, and attention, each considered no longer in isolation but in interaction with one another."[4] Our remembrance of events, participation in events, and expectation of events to come are operating all at once in the present. We cannot understand ourselves in each passing moment apart from what has come before, what is, and our expectations of what is to come. The means by which we synthesize this threefold present is the "poetic act of emplotment."[5]

However, the threefold present has an important quality to it. Each aspect of the threefold present is, as Aristotle admits, "an enigma."[6] What we recall in memory and what we anticipate in the future are not exact. With regard to memory, we remember events from an individualized perspective. That is, our memories are not a recollection of a series of facts; they are an "interwoven reference of history and fiction."[7] Ricœur notes that we necessarily fictionalize events based on the role we remember inhabiting in the past: agent or sufferer. Although the recollection of our past may weave together history and fiction, the events we select, consciously or not, shape our identity in the threefold present.

For Ricœur, it is essential to consider the relationship between emplotment and temporal experience in order to explain the power of narrative to shape identity. Our memories, as both history and fiction, contribute to the plots we construct in the threefold present. Plots work only if the events brought together in them relate to one another. This is where the poetic act is paramount. As Ricœur states, "It is only in virtue of poetic composition that something counts as a beginning, middle, or end. What defines the beginning is not the absence of some antecedent but the absence of necessity in the succession."[8] Only through the process of emplotment does the "intelligible spring from the accidental, the universal from the singular, the necessary of the probable from the episodic."[9] Once the plot has been artfully constructed, however, it does not operate in isolation. The plot is interacting, constantly, with the continuing self in time. Moment by moment, the plot is encountering our lived experience. As the narrated "story and the temporal character of human experience"[10] come together, the narrative self is constructed.

Let's just stop there and catch our breath for a moment. It's easy to get lost in this academic analysis, so let's put it in simpler, immediately applicable terms. In order to get a sense of who we are in this moment, Ricœur argues, we construct story lines for ourselves. We tell the story of our upbringing, our current circumstances, and our hopes and dreams all in the present moment. But the stories we construct are composed of events that we choose to pull together. And we choose these events for a reason. We choose them because (1) we feel we are either the driving force in them or the one being acted upon and (2) they have a storytelling thread that draws them together with other events. If this process of selecting and weaving together life events has a powerful bearing on our construction of identity, which Ricœur and I believe it does, then we must be very attentive to which events are getting top billing and how they are being told. Also, if our stories are held together by some kind of narrative thread, we must ask ourselves, What is the "glue" holding our story of self together?

Taking all of this together, we are each left with a big question: Are the events you are selecting in the story line of your "self" shaped by who *God* says you are? Will the abusive language you've endured stand on its own or will God's words of abiding love shape the way you weave those events into your story? Will you recall your straight-A work in light of the gifts God has given you for the sake of the world or will you include that in your story with only your hard work in mind? Will your congregation's dwindling membership be incorporated into your story by the angry few who blame the leadership or by those who process it through the lens of death and resurrection?

Caught your breath? Now back to the ivory tower . . .

The process by which emplotment occurs is Aristotle's three-fold mimesis.[11] $Mimesis_1$ is the state of existence prior to the beginning of narrative emplotment. It is "grounded in a pre-understanding of the world of action, its meaningful structures, its symbolic resources, and its temporal character."[12] It is the place of narrative identity in which we have what we believe to be a clear grasp of the way the world around us works. It is the temporal location in "which everyday praxis orders the present of the future, the present of the past, and the present of the present."[13]

In $mimesis_2$ the plot is developed. Ricœur describes this movement as opening up the "kingdom of the *as if*."[14] $Mimesis_2$ brings together the structures and symbolic resources of $mimesis_1$ and begins to make sense of them over time. A narrative begins to emerge: "The act of emplotment combines in variable proportions two temporal dimensions, one chronological and the other not. The former constitutes the episodic dimension of narrative. It characterizes the story insofar as it is made up of events. The second is the configurational dimension properly speaking, thanks to which the plot transforms the events into a story."[15] Here, narrative is born. A story that brings together the elements of everyday praxis and the self over time develops. The imagination begins to plot the interaction of memory as history and fiction, the present as a set of understandable structures and symbolic resources, and the expectation of what these events may bring into a story.

Mimesis$_3$ is the stage at which the story of the self is engaged with continuing human experience. The self continues to move forward in time and, therefore, cannot remain in mimesis$_2$. The self is engaged in the world as either an agent or a sufferer. Therefore, the self must continue to interpret her experience in light of her threefold present. The imagination continues to take the important events in which we participate in the world and plot them as history and fiction. This memory informs present attention and present anticipation of the future. Ricœur insists this endless spiral[16] of threefold mimesis is not vicious but rather a continuing opportunity to move into the future with a sense of being reborn.[17]

Time for some down-to-earth processing again. What is particularly powerful in Ricœur's analysis of threefold mimesis is how the story we have constructed for ourselves takes all sorts of things for granted. For instance, the first stage of mimesis assumes a certain way the world works. Of course, our assumptions about the ways of the world vary dramatically based on our life experience, including, but not limited to, our socioeconomic status, race, gender, geographic location, childhood household dynamics, and access to opportunities. But as children of God, we must also ask ourselves, To what extent and in what ways is God's work to create life and bring about resurrection, as the witness of the biblical narrative testifies, a part of our understanding?

For many of us, this is where the second stage of mimesis is so important. Whatever story each of us has constructed for ourselves, we in the context of our congregation have the incredible opportunity to place our story alongside the biblical narrative. Now a new kingdom opens up to us: We are not the first to despair in the face of loneliness. If we have felt without direction in the wilderness, we can be assured God has not forsaken us.

If we find ourselves unable to pay mounting medical expenses, we discover we are not enduring this as God's punishment. In fact, all sorts of story lines that we once thought were absurd are available to us by the grace and power of God. We are forgiven even when we cannot forgive ourselves. God will receive us with open arms even if we have squandered all of the gifts God has given us. And each of us is a beloved child of God even if our parents or peers or culture tells us we are unlovable.

Of course, to embrace and normalize this gift of identity as beloved children of God takes some time. The third stage of mimesis is arriving at a new understanding of ourselves in light of the ever-unfolding events we incorporate into our story line. This doesn't happen overnight. What might just nurture that newfound identity as God's beloved children, however, is our intentional engagement with the biblical narrative alongside other children of God who need to shore up their sense of self as well. Bible study, anyone?

Ricœur's work offers us an opportunity to begin looking at the construction of our identity from the ground up. What stories are shaping your identity as an individual or as a congregation? What events are you pulling together to create your story line? And most importantly, how is each significant event in your story shaped by the biblical narrative?

FROM THE CLASSROOM TO THE PEW

If Ricœur is not your bag, I have one more pastor and theologian to commend to you: a man who takes Ricœur's philosophy and places it in the realm of concrete reality, often painfully so. Emmanuel Katongole is a Ugandan Catholic priest and theologian, and he provides a crushing example of what can happen in the Christian church if it is not shaped *entirely* by the biblical narrative.

For Katongole, the power of the biblical narrative is not an abstract concept; it is an absolute imperative for the church. In his devastating and incredibly important book *Mirror to the Church: Resurrecting Faith after Genocide in Rwanda*,[18] he places a terrible burden at the feet of the church. In his view, it is precisely because the church did not proclaim the biblical narrative as *the defining narrative* for the church and the individual Christian's existence that Rwandans who had confessed Jesus as Lord participated as much in the genocide in Rwanda as those who had not. After recalling a history of Rwanda that includes narratives thrust upon the Rwandans from the West, Katongole asserts, "Apart from the story that taught Rwandans to understand themselves as Hutu and Tutsi, eternally at odds with one another, the genocide could not have happened. . . . What we are seeing is how the blood of tribalism comes to run deeper than the waters of baptism."[19] Developing a tribal sense of identity was not an accident. Rwandans came to see each other as a threat, as mortal enemies, because of the stories they were told—even as they had been faithful church participants. Katongole cuts to the heart: "Maybe the deepest tragedy of the Rwandan genocide is that Christianity didn't seem to make any difference. Rwandans performed a script that had shaped them more deeply than the biblical story had. Behind the silences of genocide, Hutus and Tutsis alike were shaped by a story that held their imaginations captive."[20] What we need, he persuasively argues, is to expand our imaginations. And that may happen only as we are engaged with *the narrative* that is able to show us an alternative. For Katongole, and for this author, that narrative is the biblical one.

Certainly, this is an extreme example of what can happen when we are shaped as God's people by a narrative other than the biblical narrative. However, I do not need to convince you that the biblical narrative is not the only one vying for our allegiance. How do we often respond when someone asks us who we are as churches? "We have a great music program." "We have fantastic youth programming." "We're very active in political advocacy." "We're a community-focused congregation." In many situations, these responses address the question our neighbors have really asked: "What does your church *do*?" But that's not the question that lies at the heart of what we're doing here, people. What we're doing here has to begin with "Who are we, people?" We must know who we are *and* articulate a clear understanding of who we are not.

Take just a moment to think of all the narratives that you have embraced throughout your life, the good and the not-so-good: the smart one, athletically gifted, completely worthless, a hopeless addict, a convicted felon, the ideal mom, successful at everything, driven to excel, just lazy, a pretty face, always a loner. Imagine the decisions you have made based on those narratives. What have you chosen to do, how have you chosen to live, as you've embraced those identities?

Now take a moment and think of all of the narratives your church or congregation has embraced, the good and the not-so-good: perpetually conflicted, owners of the beautiful campus, the church with the great pastor, the wealthy church, the poor church, the wedding church with that great center aisle. Imagine the decisions you have made based on those narratives. What have you chosen to do, how have you chosen to live, as you've embraced those identities?

This isn't a guilt trip, I promise. All of us have suffered at the hands of narratives not given by God. If we hadn't, Jesus wouldn't have had a lost sheep to find, a prodigal son to embrace, or a *kingdom of God* to usher in. At the same time, we needn't be stuck here, mired in our false narratives. God has given us one that is saturated with unrelenting love. We are who *God* says we are: a people created and sustained by God as we are brought from death to life each day by the grace of God for the sake of the world.

Now, finally, we can get to that "for the sake of the world" part. In the previous chapter, I spoke about the vision of the dry bones God gifts to Ezekiel. The bones were not without hope because God is the God who raises the dead. Sure enough, God's very Spirit is breathed into those bones. Sinews and tendons come together, and flesh is placed as a garment over them. God resurrects these bones from death's grip. But the bones were not only enlivened, left in a heap to fend for themselves. What God does next is to *place them on their feet.* They not only have the ability to breathe in and out and move around in the flesh that was gifted to them; they have the very spirit of God alive in them as they are brought to their feet. God has not given them life simply to occupy space in God's creation or to determine their own fate. God has brought life out of death in order that the Spirit would flow forth from them for the sake of the world! If we missed this gift of purpose in Ezekiel's vision, God gives us example after example, story after story, as it is proclaimed from Genesis to Revelation:

In Genesis 12, God says to Abram and Sarai, "Go from your country and your kindred and your father's house to the land that I will show you" (12:1). They are on the move as God's chosen vessels. But God does not send them without first telling them the purpose God has for them: "In you all the families of the earth shall be blessed" (Gen 12:3b). They are not called simply to carve out a life for themselves and for the benefit of their immediate circle. God has a purpose for them that will impact all the families of the earth.

Again, after God leads the Israelites out of slavery in Egypt, God does not leave them to figure out what they want to do next. They aren't given this new life to make the best of it on their own. No, through their leader Moses, God says to the people, "You have seen what I did to the Egyptians, and how I bore you on eagles' wings and brought you to myself. Now therefore, if you obey my voice and keep my covenant, you shall be my treasured possession out of all the peoples. Indeed, the whole earth is mine, but you shall be for me a priestly kingdom and a holy nation" (Exod 19:4–6a). God has given them the privilege of being God's faithful people, distinct and set apart as a holy nation. And they are a people gathered for *the purpose* of making God's will for life known among the nations. Of course, immediately after God's calling is revealed here in Exodus 19, they receive God's commandments in Exodus 20.

Again, after his resurrection in Matthew's Gospel, Jesus gathers his disciples together in Galilee. He wants them to experience his resurrected body firsthand and through this encounter to reassure them that God has fulfilled all of the promises God made to them along the way. Also important for this gathering is that they hear God's purposes for them: "Go therefore and make disciples of all nations, baptizing them in the name of the Father and of the Son and of the Holy Spirit, and teaching them to obey everything that I have commanded you" (Matt 28:19–20a). The disciples have the joy of experiencing the resurrection God has brought about, *and* they have a new purpose in this experience of resurrection life.

The author of Luke–Acts tells a similar story. The disciples are told to wait in the city for the Holy Spirit to be given to them before they make any decisions about what they will do next. They've seen and experienced the resurrection, but they have yet to receive their purpose. On the day of Jesus's ascension, they finally hear what they've been waiting for. Christ reveals their purpose: "You will be my witnesses in Jerusalem, in all Judea and Samaria, and to the ends of the earth" (Acts 1:8b).

Time and again in the biblical witness, God declares that God's children, as individuals and as a people, are *beloved*. They have been created in God's image and have received God's steadfast love and faithfulness. *And then* God gives them a purpose! God prepares, equips, and empowers God's children to be who God has made them for sake of the world. They are to live in their beloved status not as an end unto themselves but in order that all the world may know of their own belovedness in God as well. As we just heard God say in Exodus, "The whole earth is [God's]," and God's love extends to every corner.

WHO WE ARE HERE, PEOPLE!

Sometimes life in the church has remarkable similarities to Ann Miller and Stephen Sondheim's famous song from *Follies*, "I'm Still Here":

> Good times and bum times, I've seen 'em all
> And, my dear, I'm still here

Just making it as a community of faith from one year to the next, paying the bills and keeping the lights on, often feels like a tremendous achievement. We can shout with pride, "We're still here!" Today, that may be the best you can do. That's all right; we've all been there. But God has so much more in mind for us, and it begins when we remember who we are.

We are who God says we are—nothing more and certainly nothing less. God has called us by name, formed us in God's image, and delights in us. We are not the sum of the narratives that have been written *about* us by others. We are not who our parents, children, teachers, spouses, bosses, coaches, peers, government, advertisers, credit bureaus, or banks have said we are. We as congregations are not who the neighborhood, the judicatory, or the other churches in our city say we are. We are God's beloved children, and no one, including ourselves, can change or take away that truth, thanks be to God! With this identity, created and sustained by God, we live each day as forgiven sinners brought from death to life by the gift of Jesus Christ for us and for the world.

With that God-given and grace-shaped identity, God does not send us out so we might determine our own fate or leave our lives up to chance. God comes to us with a purpose: To love God and love our neighbor where God has planted us. To make disciples and to be witnesses of the resurrection God has brought about and the new life God is bringing about. To be a people at work for the sake of the world, set on our own two feet, ready on the starting blocks of the Holy Spirit to reveal the life God intends for all people rooted in God's perfect love.

How do we remember this one God-given identity and purpose when there are bills to pay, meetings to attend, and sermons to prepare? How do we remember this particular identity and purpose with all of the others competing for our allegiance? *We are reminded of who and why we are every time we gather around God's word revealed in the biblical narrative.* This narrative is *the defining narrative* of our existence into which God pours new life daily through the experience of death and resurrection.

It is not easy to hold on to this narrative above any other. We're constantly tempted to retreat to the identities that feel more comfortable even if they work destruction on our own sense of worth and lead us to decisions that work in opposition to God's purposes and will for life. We need each other and the constant prayer that God will move us to surrender to this God-given narrative each and every day. Without it, we may still be here, surviving each blow and clawing our way to our next "successful" stewardship campaign, but we won't be who *God has made us to be.*

Now we're ready. Put the theological debates and philosophical arguments off to the side. We're moving to the practical manifestations of living as a community shaped by the biblical narrative. For this, we need a preacher and all who are called and gathered in the name of Jesus Christ to proclaim Christ crucified and risen. It's go time.

5

WHAT IS GOD DOING HERE, PEOPLE?

"We see in a mirror, dimly. . . . Now I know only in part" (1 Cor 13:12). I'm always struck by these wise words from the apostle Paul because they seem to contradict so much of what he says elsewhere. After all, he's the one who implores the church at Corinth to "be imitators of [him]" (1 Cor 4:16). He also claims to "have become all things to all people" (1 Cor 9:22b) for the sake of the gospel. He is so very confident in his abilities as an apostle, yet he also admits freely that he cannot see the whole picture and does not fully know the mind of God. As much as Paul's words often confound me, his work in 1 Corinthians provides the language and perspective we need to begin to understand who we are as God's beloved children, shaped by the biblical narrative.

You see, it takes some chutzpah to identify ourselves as God's beloved. The identities others want to assign to us, or those we have embraced for ourselves, are often not so grace filled. The vast majority of the time, these false identities have nothing to do with what God has to say or how God has chosen to be in relationship with us. So how do we get there, to embracing the identity God has given us? How do we hear God's word for us as louder than any other? And more than that, when we begin to hear and claim the identity God gifts us as beloved children, how do we know what God would have us do next?

By now, you know a couple of responses to these questions already. How do we hear God's word above any other? (1) Encountering the biblical narrative in community with one another. (2) Praying for the Spirit's guidance as we experience the biblical narrative together. And in this chapter, I invite you to consider one more way we hear God's word for us: (3) proclaiming the good news of the biblical narrative to one another.

The work of proclamation is given to every child of God, no doubt about it. We all go about the work of proclamation in different ways, but the communication of the gospel through our words and deeds is the call of every living thing. The Old Testament gives us images of trees clapping their hands in joy at the mighty deeds of God (Isa 55:12), so you can bet God has empowered you, whatever your vocations, to praise the Lord. At the same time, many of our congregations have assigned the role of proclamation during worship to one child of God in particular—the preacher. So in our exploration of the work of proclamation, the pulpit is where we begin. But trust me, the preacher's just the beginning.

The prophet Isaiah says it best: "How beautiful . . . are the feet of the messenger who announces peace, who brings good news, who announces salvation, who says to Zion, 'Your God reigns'" (Isa 52:7). The world needs preachers who bring good news and announce peace and salvation. To proclaim the reign of God is a glorious and tremendously intimidating task, and we need that proclamation now as much as ever. To be honest, I had no idea how difficult and essential this task was until I was called upon to do it. In the next couple of pages, I offer my path of discovery to this work in the hope that it may inspire not only preachers but all children of God to embrace proclamation with humility and boldness—that we all may engage in the work of discerning "What is God doing here, people?"

FROM PERFORMANCE TO CONFESSION

The world of professional jazz musicians is often unkind to vocalists. Band leaders and members make assumptions—not necessarily accurate—about their musical training, or lack thereof. Even with years of diligent study, killer sight-reading chops, and a Jagger-like ability to command the stage, a vocalist's physical appearance and professional connections are often the determining factors in landing a job. Once a job is scheduled, it's never really secured. At the last minute, the band leader's niece, wedding couple's uncle, or bar owner's new mate might easily take their place.

Then comes the performance. The vocalist needs to decide what is most important: follow the whims of the audience for this one night, blend into the background so a featured instrumentalist holds the floor, or polish up on witty banter to keep the band as well as the audience entertained. Any of these, of course, can backfire if a vocalist has misread their audience, band leader, or other bandmates. If it wasn't such a blast to sing with brilliant jazz musicians, every vocalist might just call it quits and return for their final year of law school or dental college. After ten years living the life of a jazz vocalist, I went to seminary.

Heading into my first preaching class, I thought my years in show business would make preaching a breeze. Being on stage in front of an audience and brilliant musicians is a place of absolute joy *and* incredible risk. Every movement, note, entrance, solo, and big finish is laid bare for all the world to hear and evaluate. It's a cutthroat business with all of the life-draining temptations—drugs, booze, short-lived romances, and the false reality of the stage—that can derail even the most grounded soul. And yet, as I learned quickly, my time in the spotlight was nothing compared to proclaiming a sermon each week.

I was physically ill before offering my first sermon at seminary for preaching class. Unlike many of my classmates, I was new to this line of work and hadn't given much thought as to how I would *feel* as I proclaimed God's word. I'd performed in front of countless audiences. From performing in front of thousands of people in a large auditorium to singing to a few worn-out souls in a smoky dive at bar time, I'd commanded the stage. How hard could it be to read some Bible verses, lift out a few of the most significant words and phrases, and tell people God loves them? As it turns out, the pulpit is still the most intimidating place I've ever stood and the congregation the most nerve-wracking "audience" imaginable.

In my humble opinion, a Christian congregation is one of the more beautiful human gatherings on the planet. It is, quite literally, sacred. Sitting before the preacher are real people who have been called and gathered in the name of Jesus Christ. And the lives of real people, real children of God, are complicated. Each week, the preacher's listeners may include any number of folks from any life situation: A twentysomething who had to forego his morning hygiene routine to make it to worship, a few minutes late, because the celebration of his best friend's birthday went into the wee hours. A middle-aged woman who stayed in her car for an extra fifteen minutes after arriving in the church parking lot. She's still trying to keep it together after her spouse's addiction finally took his life and left her in financial ruin. A teen who is wondering if anyone else feels as they do, unsure about their gender identity and if God will love them if they do not identify with the gender on their birth certificate. A retiree who is torn between the life they love where they are now and the ache they feel being so far from their grandkids. A young woman who has brought with her the person she's been dating for months who happens to be Muslim. She hopes her congregation embraces him as fully as she's been embraced. And then there's the visitor who isn't sure if there's a God at all.

For a jazz vocalist, the spotlight, dim bar lighting, or large wedding floral centerpieces always obscure the eyes looking back. As a preacher, you often know what's going on *behind* the eyes, with all of the joy, monotony, and devastation that moisten them, deaden them, or light them up. The congregation before the preacher is composed of people whom the preacher loves and respects as well as those who aren't too crazy about her leadership. Terrified? I certainly have been.

As a vocalist, if you miss a note, forget some lyrics, or wear navy blue when the band is in black tuxedos, you may get an earful from your bandmates, and your pride may be hurt for a few minutes, but you can be fairly certain that no one will be damaged for years to come. However, what you say in a sermon, before God and your community, those words can have significant staying power for good and for ill. Parishioners have carried scars from preachers that have lasted a lifetime. What is spoken in Christ's name, from God's word, and for God's people must never be treated lightly.

Preaching is not only an important, humbling, powerful, awe-inspiring gift from God but also the most vulnerable ministry I've ever done for all of the reasons mentioned above and one more: preaching is more than a performance; it's a confession of faith.

Cole Porter, Ira Gershwin, and Lorenz Hart were geniuses in their field, and their lyrics resonate today, nearly one hundred years after their deaths. Vocalists take the brilliant lyrics of these writers and play with them, repeat them, condense them, add to them, and work around them. But it is clear to the performer and the audience that the lyrics are still those of Porter, Gershwin, and Hart. The vocalist will always have a degree of separation from them. He'll work with them and use them. But delivering these lyrics to an audience is a performance, and the vocalist is playing a role. When it comes to Isaiah, Ruth, Esther, Matthew, Mark, Luke, and John, the lines between written word and proclamation are not so clear.

When the psalmist writes "The Lord is my shepherd, I shall not want" (Ps 23:1), she writes not to perform but to confess. She is not constructing a fictional world to be inhabited by a heartsick ingénue or brassy belter. She is writing of her own life and experience, equipped and empowered by the Holy Spirit. The Lord has made it possible for her to walk, without fear, through the valley of the shadow of death! And when the preacher approaches these words, she does so not as a performer but as another child of God equipped and empowered by that same Holy Spirit. She hears them in the context of her own life, her own experience, *and* the lives of her parishioners. She is not detached from these words, working with them for a moment and then setting them aside. These words are part of her vocabulary of faith, even part of her confession, through which God works for the building up of the body of Christ where she is. And proclaiming that confession that has been on the lips of God's children from generation to generation, friends in Christ, is the greatest rush in the world.

Even as this preaching gig is the greatest of challenges, with profound vulnerability necessary in each preaching event, every preacher has a unique and humbling opportunity. She has, in fact, the glorious privilege to take the Spirit-inspired and Spirit-given words of the biblical narrative, words of lament in death and hope and purpose in resurrection, and proclaim *what God is doing in the midst of that congregation and how God is shaping them as God's beloved people for the sake of the world.*

On so many days and in so very many ways, proclaiming the word of God to the people of God is a downright impossible task. How could anyone reach a room full of people with such vastly different life situations? How could anyone risk the vulnerability needed to offer their confession week in and week out? How could a flawed, insecure, imperfect child of God with a sketchy history ever be the preacher God needs to let a congregation know what God is doing here? As much as these questions may dominate a preacher's thoughts, what is most certainly true is that by God's grace, *God has not left the work of preaching up to the preacher, thanks be to God!* The preacher does the work of listening, praying, reading, researching, watching, and discerning all in the presence of and under the power of the Holy Spirit! Many preachers, myself included, forget this. We must remember (and be reminded by the congregations we serve) that we prepare for the preaching event, and then God takes the message where it needs to go. Because God is merciful, slow to anger, and abounding in steadfast love, God chooses to work through us for God's purposes of love and healing, reconciliation and hope. What you say, hardworking and vulnerable preacher, matters. With all of my second-guessing, sweaty palms, and feelings of inadequacy, my congregants have said things like this about my preaching:[1]

You have challenged us to look at God's Spirit at work around us and throughout the world with wonder.

There are many times you have made me tie together the readings and my life.

I have come to note a great deal of love in the Old Testament. . . . God is with us and helps us and loves us. . . . Those who were tired and ready to give up, but God lifted them up.[2]

You may have surmised, correctly, that I take the task of preaching very seriously. But I am certainly not the best preacher in the world. Still, my preaching means a great deal to the congregation I serve, and the Holy Spirit has worked through my often-fumbling attempts to communicate the persistent presence of the grace-filled God who brings us from death to life. Your congregation needs you, and the congregation is with you in it! We, every single beloved child of God, are called to the work of the building up of the body of Christ, and what better way to do it than through our shared experience of proclaiming the Word. And make no mistake, the preaching event is not all about the preacher. Remember those incredible folks at Grace Church (GC)? They taught me that as much as they appreciate me as their Sunday morning preacher, it's really not all about me.

COURAGEOUS TOGETHER

People of God, we are all in this vocation of proclamation together. The preacher has a calling to proclaim God's word before the gathered community in all of her vulnerability and confessional witness, but we are a whole people in need of the inbreaking spirit of God through the word. The preacher's words are a beginning, an invitation, and an opening each week for her and the congregation *to consider together* what God is doing in their midst. Each and every one of us is given the biblical narrative with the constant refrain of death and resurrection in order that we may discern together what God is doing here. We are learning together, praying together, and watching for the movement of the Holy Spirit together. The people of GC have taught me, by the power of their words, the importance of communicating my need for the good news as I stand alongside them:

> As a pastor, I hear clearly that you use the pronoun "we." . . . It is clear you are part of our community and thankful for being with us.

> Pastor Rachael always preaches and teaches with us. . . . She normally preaches as just another believer in God.

> You definitely convey your belief that we are [GC] congregation together. You're totally "in it" with us.[3]

We, all of us, need a word from God that speaks to us where we are, whether we are standing on the pulpit or sitting in the pew. We need someone to announce peace and salvation and proclaim to us that our God reigns. We may see in a mirror dimly, but God has given us so much to see! The biblical witness is packed with images, stories, people, and places that invite us to see ourselves and our communities in them. They speak to us where we are in joy and suffering, in hope and despair. We need all of it, every word and phrase, every metaphor, parable, and command, to lead us to see God's presence among us. As we proclaim the gospel of death and resurrection to one another, God places before us all the words we need.

WE HAVE THE WORDS

Not long into my tenure with the people of GC, I saw what an impact the language of the biblical witness could have in helping a congregation talk about what they were going through. In their encounters with Scripture together, the words of the Old and New Testament witness had become more and more familiar to them. They felt increasingly at home in the language of the biblical narrative, and it was becoming more natural for them to understand their congregational story as woven into it. The Psalms and the wilderness experiences of God's people came up again and again in our conversations. But a few members of the congregation identified with much more of what God's people had experienced in generations past, more than the beautiful Psalms and wilderness struggles that come up frequently on a Sunday morning. Particularly striking to me was one member's reference to a more obscure image: "So, I think, when the Israelites were in exile and referred to as a scattered remnant, I thought we were a scattered remnant."[4] This language makes so much sense to our congregations and to preachers, but we don't often dig that deep. Actually, we can't dig that deep unless we're reading even more of the biblical witness than what is assigned for worship.

That rich and deep resource of the totality of Scripture was available to all of us at GC, yet we were just beginning to explore everything the biblical narrative had to offer. When I arrived, many in the congregation had already been making their way through glorious scriptural territory, but most of their journey had been on well-worn paths: the Gospels, the stories of Abraham and Moses, and the like. I quickly began to wonder, What might we learn together about what God is doing among us if we develop an even deeper connection with Scripture? If we get to know it better together? GC had grown so much already in their study of Scripture. Where else in the biblical narrative might God reach us and teach us? So I took a chance. I asked them to set off with me on a walk through the whole biblical witness, Genesis through Revelation.

I'm no expert on leadership theory when it comes to congregational life, but I know congregations often give pastors an extra measure of grace in their first weeks and months on the job. A little less than a year into my ministry with GC, I decided to cash in all of my chips, throw caution to the wind, and make my way through the directory, calling each member. I asked them one question: "Would you meet with me and other members of GC once a week for the next year to study the Bible?" A friend had introduced me to Brian McLaren's book *We Make the Road by Walking*, which provided a guide for engaging the arc of the whole biblical witness in one year. Many familiar passages were addressed, but it would also take us into scriptural places many had not yet gone. By the grace of God, it was the perfect tool to launch us on a new adventure in the Spirit.

We welcomed only about sixty-five people in worship at the time, so it didn't take me more than a few days to call everyone and invite them to be a part of our year of Bible study. But the results were staggering: forty-three of the sixty-five members I contacted were in! And, spoiler alert, around thirty-eight of them stuck with it for the whole year! All of the work and study the congregation had been doing before I arrived did not make them weary of engagement with the Bible; they wanted more. They could see how the story was speaking to them, about them, and in them. As their engagement with Scripture empowered them to see how more and more people in the Bible were strikingly similar to them, I was emboldened to make connections between these stories and our congregation. We trusted one another with our stories. And soon it became clear that we, pastor and congregation, had much in common with the biblical witness. This was especially true when we embraced, together, the practice of lament.

We discussed early in our study together that we felt a sense of sadness, anger, and powerlessness in our neighborhood. We saw so much violence, drug use, and poverty we didn't know how to respond (more on that in chapters 6 and 7). Church members spoke openly about the congregational projects they had tried and ministries they had initiated in years past to serve their neighbors in need. But each of these attempts brought more division than healing, and the neighborhood just wasn't getting better. Many were motivated by Matthew 25:40: "Truly I tell you, just as you did it to one of the least of these who are members of my family, you did it to me." It's good to be motivated by that verse. I believe it was Jesus's intent to move us with those words to love and serve our neighbor. These words are so popular, in fact, that you can find any number of cross-stitch patterns, banners, and mugs displaying them in bright, inviting colors. Less known, however, are these words from the same Gospel: "When [Jesus] saw the crowds, he had compassion for them, because they were harassed and helpless, like sheep without a shepherd" (Matt 9:36). Even with Jesus's ability to heal, he was still deeply moved by the suffering he saw around him. Even though he could take away the pain of those he saw, it did not erase what he witnessed: a harassed and helpless people.

I had been able to have beautiful conversations around the witness of Scripture with many members of the congregation through our time of Bible study. When hearing Hannah's story, a young couple shared their deep grief over their inability to have children. When studying the prophet Joel chapter 2, a man was bold to share a vision he had had while in worship at GC some time ago. When discussing Mark 1 and Jesus's work to cast out demons, a woman in recovery shared that her experience in the throes of addiction felt much like a kind of demon possession. Because the people of GC had been open with me about the intersection of their lives and the biblical narrative, I decided to take a risk when the Luke 9, "harassed and helpless" passage was appointed for worship and offer an example about myself.

Just that week, our parking lot had been the site of an awful domestic dispute. I did not recognize the couple involved; they were unsheltered neighbors and carried on their bodies the clear markings of drug addiction. I wanted desperately to help, but I didn't have the skills. I walked outside and called to them to let the aggressor know he was being watched. I was told, in direct fashion, that I was not wanted or needed. I was very concerned for the safety of the other member of the couple, so I dialed 911. I knew from experience and the added frustration of an under-staffed police department that no one would be coming any time soon. By the time the police did arrive, some thirty minutes later, one child of God was lying bloodied on the pavement, and the other was nowhere to be found. I felt sick to my stomach and utterly useless. How could I, how could we as a congregation, be a force for good? I asked that question in my sermon.

I remember it well, although it was more than a few years ago, because I'd never been that vulnerable in front of a congregation before. I had never allowed myself to stand before a congregation and without reservation state my own feelings of powerlessness. I had never proclaimed that I had no idea how to lead the congregation in addressing the needs of our neighbors. But as it turned out, it helped all of us connect the feelings and actions of Jesus from two thousand years ago to what he would see and undoubtedly feel looking at our neighborhood that week. We all—the violent couple, the helpless pastor, and the congregation that heard about the most recent police activity on our property—needed a shepherd that day in worship. We needed compassion, and we needed it, all of us, from the one who saw us in our grief; who proclaimed a new kingdom marked by forgiveness, mercy, and love; and who would go to the cross as our Savior. We needed Jesus, and in that moment of proclamation, pastor and congregation received the grace only our Lord may provide.

While I was unsure about the wisdom of making myself that vulnerable with my congregation as their pastoral leader and preacher, the response was overwhelmingly positive. Through this experience with the people of GC, I learned that not only can I be honest with the congregation about my personal feelings of grief, but sharing our lament with one another allows us to grow in trusted relationship. Knowing that I, *the pastor*, was struggling with grief over the brokenness in our neighborhood, a number of other leaders felt comfortable speaking openly about their grief as well. It gave the congregation the opportunity simply to grieve and not have to find a way to fix it. Sharing this deep sadness with each other gave us permission to be God's people who see in a mirror dimly and know only in part.

In all honesty, I don't think it will ever be comfortable for me to be so honest and open about what is tough for me in my walk of faith. But this call to preaching was never meant to be comfortable. Amen?! We, pastors and congregations, are in this together, and we need each other to speak what is real as we discern together how God is at work in relationship with us and the world. What is God doing here, people? God is our shepherd, our comforter, and our Savior. On many a Sunday morning, that's our witness and testimony. What a necessary and glorious calling!

The Bible gives us, preacher and people, the words to name who we are as God's beloved children in God's constant presence. These words proclaim God's limitless love for a broken world and, finally, reassure us of God's ability to do something about it. If and when we risk the vulnerability required to speak our lament and use the words of Scripture to guide us, we are led exactly where we need to go. We are harassed and helpless, but we are not left without a shepherd. And our shepherd destroyed the power of death forever.

THE GOOD NEWS IS REALLY GOOD

Are you ready for the payoff? As a proclaimer of God's word, I cannot imagine anything better. When we allow Scripture to lead us to voice the lament we are already feeling, the experience of death in our daily living, the good news is about as good as it gets. On the heels of that experience of lament in the face of death, we, pastors and congregations, have the humbling privilege to proclaim the truth that God refuses to leave us there! As we become a people who are able to see and name the lament, we become a people on the lookout for resurrection.

Language for this, too, is provided in abundance in the biblical witness. From Miriam's song in Exodus, "Sing to the Lord, for he has triumphed gloriously; horse and rider he has thrown into the sea" (15:21), to the shout of a forgiving father in the Gospel of Luke, "For this son of mine was dead and is alive again; he was lost and is found" (15:24a), we have no shortage of language to point to and celebrate resurrection life.

Recently, in the midst of the Covid pandemic, I was able to stand before my people and proclaim the words of Paul and Timothy to the church at Corinth: "Our hope for you is unshaken; for we know that as you share in our sufferings, so also you share in our consolation. We do not want you to be unaware, brothers and sisters, of the affliction we experienced in Asia; for we were so utterly, unbearably crushed that we despaired of life itself. Indeed, we felt that we had received the sentence of death so that we would rely not on ourselves but on *God who raises the dead*" (2 Cor 1:7–9; italics added). Every one of us, in one way or another, was feeling unbearably crushed. Alongside people around the world, we were trying to find a way to keep moving forward after endless losses. We lost loved ones and were unable to mourn them as a community, lost jobs or were dealing with diminished household incomes, faced escalating manifestations of mental illness in ourselves and others, lost graduation celebrations and wedding gatherings, and experienced the oppressive anxiety that came with trying to help our kids learn something at home while parents were doing what they could to keep up with work. All of this was happening with the backdrop of a bitterly divisive political culture and the exposure of our nation's historical and contemporary complicity in systemic racism. It was too much for all of us. As days stretched into weeks, and weeks into months, the sense of hopelessness threatened to consume us.

Yet as God's word was proclaimed in our worship, we heard that Paul and Timothy's hope was unshaken! They had hope not because they would never suffer again or because of some notion that "where God closes a door, God opens a window." They had hope because *God raises the dead!* For many of us, the witness of Paul and Timothy came at just the right moment (imagine that!). We needed to remember that the very real death and loss we each were experiencing would not have the final word! God was with us, holding us and carrying us. God would not stand by uninterested as we sank deeper into despair. God was reaching over the thousands of years and countless miles between us and Paul and Timothy to bring us the good news we needed: God raises the dead! There is hope! We spent the rest of the sermon time, and plenty of time after worship, naming for one another where new life was springing up in our city and in our own lives. As we shared our glimpses of God's resurrection life, we were given food for the journey. Our mourning turned to dancing in that time of worship, and we were fortified to be God's vessels of love and light for one more week—just long enough to make it until we heard the good news together again.

As we develop this vocabulary of resurrection life, a vocabulary spoken and lived out for us in the biblical narrative and witness, it becomes the way in which we describe *our own story*. We begin to understand our story as one that is woven into the glorious, grand narrative of the Bible that has been given to us over the generations. For the people of GC, God's work of resurrection in the life of their congregation over the years of hardship has been miraculous, with deep resonances with the biblical witness. Two members used stories from that witness to describe their own experience:

[Grace Church]'s story mirrors the story of the Israelites falling away from, from living close to God and what God wants for us. But then being restored and we're in a state of being more restored now but that God has been with us.[5]

I'm going to use Lazarus's story. I kind of feel like we're rising from the tomb. You know, we've been covered up for so long. Now it's time to take the rags off.[6]

When the preacher and the congregation are bold to proclaim the new resurrection life God provides in the language of the biblical narrative, the old, old story of God's persistent love for all creation flies on the wings of the Spirit and *is revealed as our story.* We are given hope that the God of heaven and earth who has created, sustained, equipped, empowered, and resurrected God's people from generation to generation will continue that glorious work for and in us! Then as God's people, we are given the purpose to be a part of God's grace-filled work wherever God leads us! We must not hold back. We must proclaim our deep sadness, anger, and frustration as helpless and harassed sheep *and* allow the God of resurrection life to remind us that it is never over until Christ reigns over all. This is the humbling privilege, blessing, and utter joy of proclaiming the biblical witness as pastor and people. Hallelujah!

GET READY

All that being said, I would be remiss not to offer one caution, or as my son might say, one "heads-up." As you proclaim and embrace this biblical narrative that moves us from honest, vulnerable lament to the God who raises the dead, be ready. Everything will change. You may be assuming that I'm putting hyperbole to some good use here. "C'mon," you might say. "How could proclaiming death and resurrection possibly change *everything*?" Your question may be valid. You may be further down the road than I was when my congregation taught me about the power of the biblical narrative to shape us as God's people. But consider yourself warned! Preaching and hearing the biblical narrative of death and resurrection as the overarching story that tells us who we are in God's beloved world can take over quickly. And congregations on the lookout for resurrection are fierce forces for the gospel!

For the preacher of a resurrection-looking congregation, prayer and study with the people become more important than hours alone reading in the office. Conversations in the neighborhood provide more insight into the biblical text than your favorite sermon prep podcast. Don't get me wrong; individual study and podcasts are important tools. They certainly are in my preparation. Yet as the congregation shifts from business as usual to a focus on the movement of the Spirit that brings us through death to life, God's work in your midst—and in the midst of the congregation—increasingly becomes the driving force behind what you choose to say, how you choose to spend your time, and how you understand your role in the life of the congregation. It is God who shows us who we are, gives us our reason for being, and sends us out to be a people who are daily brought from death to life. As one bold preacher brilliantly proclaims, "Preaching is the ultimate vocation because at this the end of the age when so many sit stupefied and traumatized, the word gives power to those who hear and to those who speak. It will save your life."[7]

Take courage preachers, congregations, and all who proclaim the gospel of death and resurrection. God is bringing us to new life! Now get ready, because God's just getting started!

6

HOW ARE WE *LIVING* WHAT GOD'S DOING HERE, PEOPLE?

On the occasion of my father's receiving his driver's license, his father wrote him a letter. It spoke of the great responsibility of operating a motor vehicle. It may sound remarkably old school, a father in the early 1960s writing a letter to his son rather than discussing the subject over the dining room table. But I couldn't be more grateful that his words have been preserved. The letter is loaded with wisdom, the kind of wisdom that transcends the subject. The words are carefully chosen and are, perhaps, more relevant today than they were nearly sixty years ago. Of particular interest to us as Jesus followers is the section on what would be at stake if this new driver decided to raise some hell behind the wheel. After a brief discussion about the financial ramifications of driving while raising hell, my grandfather moves into more significant territory: "Our good name and personal honor rest on your shoulders as well as ours—never more so than when you're driving our car. I'll spare you any faltering attempts to express the love your mother and I bear for you or our constant concern for your safety. Just keep in mind that everybody is loved by someone—I mean the person driving with you, or behind you, or in front, or on foot in the path of your car. A lot of responsibility to hand out, isn't it?" Boom. My grandfather did not mince words about the responsibility of driving a car.

I've wondered a number of times if a letter like this might be helpful for our faith communities. Many of us churchgoers are aware of our shortcomings. We know we have, as Paul says, fallen short of the glory of God (Rom 3:23). We know we have not lived up to Jesus's call in the Gospel of John to love one another as Christ loved us (15:12). It's almost embarrassing to sing the old favorite "They Will Know We Are Christians by Our Love." Certainly, the love of God has shone through faith communities throughout the generations, in intimate relationships, and when we have worked together for the common good. It's just that our inability to love one another is often so very public, stubborn, and damaging. When we decide to raise hell as congregations, the aftereffects linger for generations and often alienate those Jesus made his priority—the marginalized, ostracized, excluded, and struggling.

Some may think it is unfair that a congregation called and gathered in Christ's name would bear responsibility for Christ's name in the world. Or in the words of my grandfather, that Christ's name would rest on our shoulders. We are human, aren't we? I feel the weight of that responsibility daily. I question, quite often, God's move in Christ to entrust us with the message of reconciliation (2 Cor 5:19). Why in heaven and on earth did

God decide to do that? From where I sit, with my own life in view, I can imagine God wants a take-back on that decision every day of the week.

But no matter my opinion or yours, bearing the name of Christ Jesus inside and outside of the church is what we do. It isn't fair, and our salvation doesn't rest on our doing it well, thanks be to God. But ultimately, it moves us to ask, "If we are beloved children of God, shaped by God's word, which leads us from death to resurrection, and made new in that word for the sake of the world, how do we begin to live that truth?" That question is the focus of this chapter.

Living as a people being made new daily for the sake of the world is our call. It's also impossible for us to do on our own. What we need to remember, right out of the gate, is that to live as God's people cannot be our project; it *must be (and is) God's project*. Our daily way of being as God's people must be about God's will and God's purposes. *This project, God's will be done, is the project in which we participate by God's grace.* No wonder Jesus taught us to pray daily, God's will be done. The people of Grace Church (GC) have modeled this way of being as God's people, and they continue to teach me. The ways in which they place the emphasis on God's will and not our own are too many to name here. However, three foundational pieces rest beneath them all: prayer, forgiveness, and imagination.

LORD, WE NEED TO HEAR FROM YOU

One of the best Andraé Crouch songs in his brilliant catalog is entitled "We Need to Hear from You." The song begins with this direct address to God and then poses the question, "If we don't hear from you, Lord, what will we do?" Amen, brother. It is God who determines what we will do because it is in *God* that we live and move and have our being.

Yet how many of our budget meetings, evangelism meetings, and worship meetings are bathed in prayer, asking God how *God* would have us live and serve together? Before I arrived at GC, I always began meetings with the obligatory "opening prayer" listed at the top of the agenda. But I admit I didn't spend much time praying over the agenda, asking for God's guidance, or listening for God's voice before, during, and after these meetings. I also didn't ask other members of the congregation to hold those meetings in prayer, not trusting that their prayers for us made a difference. To be a people rooted in communication with God takes time, patience, and a willingness to admit that without God's guidance, we don't stand a chance of moving into the future *God* has in mind for us. It means being open to the presence of God in the lives of everyone around the table and the very real possibility that God may just have revealed the congregation's next move to the person who has the least to say. It means being prepared for open-ended conversation and allowing time to discern the movement of God's spirit rather than making a decision about each agenda item in order to get through it expeditiously. I can't tell you how difficult that can be for me. I like to keep things moving, take action, and feel like we're making progress through the agenda items that have been set before us. But I've had to ask myself, What kind of progress am I making, in what direction am I moving, if the plan is mine and not God's?

As my mind, body, and spirit have been opened to this prayerful way of being, I see how it comes up again and again in Scripture. Shocking, right, that God's will would be made known as God's children *talk with and listen to God*? I can be a little slow on the uptake. But because God's will is so often in direct opposition to ours, we need to listen to and hear from God to determine what the right path is. I just love the stories of God's servants who go the way they choose only to be redirected in subtle and not-so-subtle ways to the path God would have them walk. Some obvious examples are Jonah, who fled to Tarshish, and Moses, who refused to be God's instrument (with subsequent negotiations). Jesus insists that the disciples not do anything until they've been given the Holy Spirit: "And see, I am sending upon you what my Father promised; so *stay here* in the city until you have been clothed with power from on high" (Luke 24:49; italics added).

But lately, my favorite story is a more obscure passage from the Prophets. It's tucked into Jeremiah, a book that states plainly the prophet Jeremiah's contentious relationship with God. This story resonates with my experience as one child of God called to be a part of God's project and the prayer that is required to do it. The story begins: "In the fourth year of King Jehoiakim son of Josiah of Judah, this word came to Jeremiah from the Lord: Take a scroll and write on it all the words that I have spoken to you against Israel and Judah and all the nations, from the day I spoke to you, from the days of Josiah until today. It may be that when the house of Judah hears of all the disasters that I intend to do to them, all of them may turn from their evil ways, so that I may forgive their iniquity and their sin" (Jer 36:1–3). Let's just stop there for a moment. Jeremiah, beloved child of God, is called upon by God to write down on a scroll (actually Baruch, Jeremiah's scribe, does the writing) all of the horrible things God is going to do to Judah because of Judah's unjust and unfaithful deeds. Jeremiah is then to take this scroll and read it out to the people of Judah in the town square. Already sounds like a fun project, doesn't it? Anyone think their congregational leaders would decide this was a good idea or place it on the church board's agenda for a vote? But what comes next is just brutal.

The king, Jehoiakim, hears of this infamous scroll, as it is causing quite a stir in the streets of Judah. The king calls on a servant, Jehudi, to bring the scroll to him and read it aloud: "Now the king was sitting in his winter apartment (it was the ninth month), and there was a fire burning in the brazier before him. As Jehudi read three or four columns, the king would cut them off with a penknife and throw them into the fire in the brazier, until the entire scroll was consumed. . . . And the king commanded Jerahmeel the king's son and Seraiah son of Azriel and Shelemiah son of Abdeel to arrest the secretary Baruch and the prophet Jeremiah. But the Lord hid them" (Jer 36:22–23, 26). Can you feel the tension in the room? The warmth of the fire is mixed with the king's rising rage as beads of sweat collect on his royal forehead. And what about all of those servants and advisors around the king? Can you imagine what a great story they'd have to share over dinner when their spouses asked, "So how was work today, honey?" Still, my favorite part is yet to come.

With Jeremiah and Baruch in hiding from the king's arrest order, the word of God comes to them again. What could God possibly want now? Without a doubt, the wisest course of action would be for Jeremiah and Baruch to lay low. But that's not God's will. God has the whole people of Judah in mind, so God commands the one, essential course of action— Jeremiah and Baruch must write God's word out all over again: "The word of the Lord came to Jeremiah: Take another scroll and write on it all the former words that were in the first scroll, which King Jehoiakim of Judah has burned" (Jer 36:27b–28). God's course may quite easily be described as reckless, stubborn, and a drain on both human and material resources. And it's what God wills.

This beautiful passage from the life of Jeremiah also has everything to do with being a part of God's project as we discern God's will and way in conversation with God. Not many of us are called to the frightening, constantly confrontational, in-the-halls-of-power kind of ministry that Jeremiah endured, thanks be to God. However, this episode reflects much of what we are called to be about as God's people. And the simple fact is that what God calls us to do may be discerned only in daily prayer and conversation with God. For example, Jeremiah and Baruch's ministry stood in opposition to the status quo. They were called to speak and act for the radical changes needed in their community. All we need to do is walk around our neighborhoods to see such changes are necessary right now. Poverty, addiction, lack of access to health care and adequate nutrition, limited opportunities, systemic racism—all are on full display. The question is not *if* God is calling us to speak out and act in opposition to the status quo; it is *how*. Maybe your congregation has access to the halls of power, thanks be to God! What direction might God lead you if you are all praying about that together? Maybe your congregation is in an economically depressed area. What opportunities might open up for your ministry if you are all praying together about how and where to serve? Maybe you're in a small town that is dealing with the effects of the opioid epidemic. To what action might God move you if you all pray together about what God's will is for your congregation in the midst of that community? The people of GC have taught me that when God places you in a neighborhood, God will equip you to serve it. The question is, Will you pray together to listen for *how* God is leading you?

Second, whatever resources you have are all for God's purposes. The question is, *How are we to use them?* Do you see a theme developing here? I certainly did. The scroll Baruch and

Jeremiah created would have taken hours and hours, most likely days, to complete. The papyrus upon which they wrote would not have been cheap. Then they were called to use their voices, stand before the people, and speak. This undertaking was paid for in human and material currency. When that costly labor reached the king, it all went up in smoke, quite literally, in a matter of minutes. That had to sting for both Jeremiah and Baruch. It hurts me just thinking about it. Not many congregations are rolling in human or financial resources right now. Amen? We're doing everything we can to be responsible with the resources God has entrusted to us. Yet when we're in conversation with God, it is astounding how quickly and, with what seems like reckless abandon, how generously God desires to spread those resources around. How has your congregation been doing in asking for God's will to be done with the resources you've been entrusted? My prayer has been, far too often, *Please give us what we need.* In prayer, God calls us to ask, *How can we put to use what you've given us for your purposes?*

Finally—and the most inspiring for me in this reading—is God's clear instruction to Jeremiah and Baruch that when they get pushed down doing the work of God, they will be called and given the strength to get back up. God's servants had been dismissed, silenced, and threatened. Jeremiah and Baruch were shut down and told to stay down. But God comes to them, in their experience of death itself, and called them to life again. As we follow God and discern God's path for us, we're going to get pushed down. For many of our congregations, it's a question not of when but of how many times we've hit the dirt. It's not going to stop any time soon. Our Savior proclaims,

Blessed are the poor in spirit, for theirs is the kingdom of heaven.

Blessed are those who mourn, for they will be comforted.
Blessed are the meek, for they will inherit the earth.
(Matt 5:3–5)

And this Savior is not going to help us find the path of least resistance. God calls us to love one another and love our neighbor as ourselves. Love makes us vulnerable to loss, to grief, and to all sorts of pushback from the powers that work against God in the world and in ourselves. We will get knocked down following this Christ. *And* Christ will give us strength to get back up again. Especially when we've been knocked down, we need to hear from God. We need a word from God. And by the grace of God, God's calendar always has room for us, anywhere at any time.

As a congregation, the people of GC pray. They pray out loud with and for each other. They pray before, during, and after meetings. They pray individually at scheduled times throughout the day. They encourage their pastor to pray by offering her time away from church for the express purpose of being in conversation with God. We need to hear from God every moment of every day in order that we may be a part of God's project, that God's will be done. Amen?

FORGIVE ME BECAUSE
I DON'T KNOW WHAT I'M DOING

When a community lives day to day discerning what God would have them do, they see, as the apostle Paul says, in a mirror dimly (1 Cor 13:12). Certainty is elusive at best and a seductive illusion at worst. Apart from the gift of God's grace and the love we have been given through our Lord Jesus Christ, our lives remain a mystery. Still, we are called by God to make bold decisions for the sake of the gospel and to take all sorts of risks in order that we might reach our neighbor with the love of Christ. We are to build up the body of Christ and serve our Lord who proclaims unequivocally, "And I, when I am lifted up from the earth, will draw all people to myself" (John 12:32). Christ's vision is expansive, including all the earth. Ours must be as well. With this all-encompassing, boldness-requiring, dimly lit call, we must move into God's future *with full awareness that we are not going to get it right every time.* We pray for God's direction because we know we are not called to move out on our own, and we are clear about our limited powers of discernment. I'm still waiting for that red phone to Jesus. If you see one on the market, let me know.

In this environment of (1) taking risks for the sake of the gospel while (2) knowing that taking risks may lead us in the wrong direction, the people of GC have shown me that the only way to thrive in the midst of it all is to cover the whole undertaking in grace-filled forgiveness. The pastor can be an easy target when congregations start talking about getting things wrong. But for the sake of illustrating the argument, I'll go ahead and share two of the ways forgiveness is mandatory in the faith community by laying before you how I've gotten it wrong and needed the forgiveness of the community.

First, I have on more than one occasion felt God was calling us in a direction that time revealed was the wrong way. One example should suffice. As I mentioned earlier, in my first year at GC, we were struggling in our relationship with our preschool. One point of conflict was the extent to which God and faith should be discussed during the course of daily instruction. The church had become disconnected from the preschool ministry, and we desperately wanted to build that relationship. Through the preschool director, I was introduced to, in my opinion, a faithful and gifted teacher who wanted to expand the school to include early elementary grades. Her main focus was to weave the biblical stories into everyday education. In my mind, that was it! She was just what we had been looking for! With her leadership, we could begin to steer this school ship in the right direction. I asked this wonderful woman to put together a formal proposal for this expansion of our preschool for the next congregational board meeting about a month away. The project must have taken her the better part of the entire month, because the proposal was beautiful. It contained financial estimates, including costs to the congregation and costs incurred by prospective families. It provided a sample science lesson in which the creation stories of Genesis 1 and 2 were set alongside modern scientific teachings about the beginning of life on earth. She talked about the space she needed in the building and where she could, with the least obstruction to our current ministries, hold the classes. I was beyond excited to present this proposal to the congregational leadership. Surely, like me, they could see this was exactly what God wanted us to do.

You can anticipate where this is going, can't you? Not only was the council not excited about the proposal, but by the end of our council meeting, they were in full agreement: this was not what they felt God was calling us to do. I was floored. Couldn't they see this was an answer to prayer? Of course, they had very good reasons not to move forward. The use of space would make our building inaccessible to some of the outside groups, including AA and NA, which had been important resources for our community for years. Tuition for the preschool was expensive, and the early elementary grades would need to be costly as well, at least for the first couple of years. In all likelihood, people in our immediate neighborhood could not afford to send their students to the school. The preschool had been established originally because no public kindergarten was available. This would further divide families into different school systems, public and private, which seemed to conflict with our ongoing support for the local public elementary school just up the street. The vote was unanimous against the proposal I had brought. The only deviation was my abstention.

If I'm honest, I was completely surprised and more than a little disappointed. I trusted God was at work in and through this group of gifted and faithful leaders, *and* I was pretty sure I was right. Yet it would only take about six months, a whirlwind of unexpected changes, and the unimaginable closure of our preschool for me to see and begin to understand *just how wrong I was.* God had placed our congregation on a path, and in relationship with a new nonprofit (see chapter 2), that required the full use of our building. Had we expanded the school, we would have added another layer of complexity and grief to an already confusing and often painful transition when the preschool began to fall apart.

I hadn't shared my disappointment over the rejection of the school proposal. I was very new to the congregation and had immediately become a cheerleader for them as they supported me and my ministry at every turn. But I was the first to say how happy I was that we hadn't moved forward with the proposal *after* the events of that summer. I can say that with such confidence and remember it so well because of one grace-filled fact: no one felt the need to remind me that I had made an incorrect judgment. Consider that for a moment. Everyone on that council, looking back at the school proposal, could have taken the opportunity to point out, "Hey, pastor, do you remember when you wanted us to expand the school? Boy, that would have been catastrophic! What a relief we didn't listen to you!" But no one did. I have mentioned a number of times since then how wise they were not to listen to me, but they never have. They knew we were all doing our very best to love God and love one another. They knew I was praying about everything, just like they were. They knew that our disagreement over what to do was not because they were good Christians and I was not. We were all taking a risk—to move forward with the proposal or to vote it down—while seeing in a mirror dimly. They forgave my stubbornness and misguided certainty, and we've been moving on together ever since.

I wish that was the only time I needed their forgiveness, but truth be told, there are too many instances to recall. Just one more overall category of forgiveness-requiring actions seems necessary to mention, however. Again, when you're all flying by the seat of your pants on the winds of the Spirit, solid footing is impossible. You're always a little unsteady, always responding instead of planning, and always pushed to the edges of your ability to process it all. For me, particularly when the Spirit is moving quickly and I can't quite keep up, the first thing to go is my memory. Now if I forgot a birthday, unknowingly blew off a meeting, or missed a retirement party, I would have been irritated to have missed out. But I've done much worse. Just imagine this:

1. You are the president of the council. Your mother passes away, and you've asked the pastor to please announce the funeral at worship the next Sunday. You sit, somewhat stunned, at the completion of the announcements at worship that week, because the pastor forgot to announce your mother's funeral service. When she asks if there are any other announcements "for the good of the community," you stand up and have to invite everyone to your own mother's funeral.

2. Your two-year-old nephew is undergoing a dangerous but necessary surgery. Your whole family is pretty worried. You've purchased a beautiful blanket to send to your nephew that you'd love for the congregation to bless at the next worship service. Your pastor is excited to be a part of a blanket blessing and tells you she'll lead the congregation in a prayer for your nephew as well so you can send the blanket off with their prayers and blessings. You hold on to that blanket all the way through worship, and when the pastor recesses out of the sanctuary at the beginning of the postlude, you realize she's completely forgotten you, your nephew, and the blanket.

Appalled yet? I would be, and I'm the pastor who did them both. Both of these mistakes on my part are inexcusable. Both of these parishioners would be completely justified in lodging complaints about my leadership with the congregational board.

But do you know what both individuals decided to do? Forgive me. In fact, when I approached both of these women later to apologize profusely, they were quick to offer their kindness, reassurance, and affirmation of my ministry. Of course, that made me feel worse, but I trust that wasn't their intent. I'm still mortified at these mistakes, but they're not. They've moved on and have decided to trust me as their pastor as we move together into God's future. God's grace abounds. We can't do God's work without it.

WITH IMAGINATION WE'LL GET THERE

On a deep track from an old Harry Connick Jr. album is one of his great New Orleans–style gospel tunes entitled "With

Imagination I'll Get There." In the middle of the first verse, Connick tells us where he's hoping to "get." If weary is your world, he croons, there's heaven to discover. Apparently, the only thing he needs to discover that new heaven is—you guessed it—imagination. OK, so it might come across as a touch simplistic. But in significant ways, Connick's insightful lyrics name the final foundational piece upon which the ministry of GC stands.

We've come to discover something rather beautiful in our ministry together at GC: God's ideas are always bigger than ours. That's not to say God's ideas must take a lot of time and resources or involve a lot of people. But what God dreams up always blows our minds because God can imagine and so create beyond our wildest expectations. As we live into who God shapes us to be, we become something different from what any of us could have imagined. This is glorious, astounding good news *if* we are open to expanding our own imaginations as well.

Our congregation had been praying for some time about the poverty in our neighborhood. Jesus's call to serve "the least of these" (Matt 25:40) resonated profoundly within and among us. Through an advocacy event hosted by our congregation, we were introduced to the practice of predatory lending and the devastating consequences of being trapped in a loan with terms including up to 1,000 percent interest (nope, I'm not exaggerating). Many of us were incensed, but what could we do? Sure, we'd work through our legislators to try to establish a cap for these loans. But after some prayer, God opened up our imaginations. What if, we asked, we could help those most vulnerable to the predatory lending industry? What if we could educate borrowers and establish a small savings account for those families living on the edge so they could build financial capacity?

It was a harebrained idea. What did we know about financial education? Only enough to be dangerous. But God seems to just love harebrained ideas. The God who created the great sea beast Leviathan for sport, who fed thousands of people with just a few loaves of bread and a handful of fish, and who wouldn't allow a wedding to continue without an ample supply of the best wine money could buy has invited us into a life of glorious imagination. God plants ideas firmly in our imaginations, and we have the opportunity to encourage them in each other. The leaders of GC told me to keep going with this idea, and I did. With a few phone calls, God introduced us to people who did know about financial education and who were working diligently and daily to help struggling families develop financial capacity. After making Christ-centered connections in the nonprofit world, and with the outward-reaching goals of a local credit union, we were on our way. With imagination, we'll get there.

One more story, because it's just so much fun. During the global pandemic, many of the local food pantries that provided for low-income families were hard hit. Almost all their volunteers, upon whom they'd relied to pack thousands of pounds of food and ready it for distribution each week, were over the age of sixty-five and unable to serve. The risk was too great. But the demand for food was on the rise as millions lost their jobs or were forced to take pay cuts. A mission partner of ours was sharing the facts of this situation with a group of our members. Out of the blue, one member said, "Well, we can do something about that, can't we? A lot of us older folks can't volunteer, but we don't need the stimulus we've been given either. What if we gave that to you, and you hired someone to help?"

I wasn't a part of this conversation, but the organizer of the group said, "It just struck me, and I said to myself, 'I think that was the Spirit speaking through her.'" Now I wish I would have simply replied "Hallelujah!" to this whole adventure. But I was a little nervous. I wondered if asking people to give to an outside organization when finances were so tight for so many might be a tremendous burden or even a slap in the face. But this group was adamant, and their Spirit-ignited imaginations were pushing us ahead. Next, they requested that I contact a couple of other congregations and ask if they'd like to help. Again, if I'm honest, I was more reluctant than excited. OK, I really didn't want to. Churches all over our city were struggling. How would they receive my request? But God again expanded my imagination through the generosity of our neighboring churches. In less than six weeks and with the participation of five different church organizations, we raised over $33,000 together. A full-time job was created, and people were fed. With imagination, we'll get there.

GET BEHIND THE WHEEL AND GO

To be God's people for the sake of the world is an extraordinary responsibility. To be a people shaped and formed by God's word of death and resurrection, to serve a God whose will is for life and love all over the earth, can easily be overwhelming. But God isn't overwhelmed. God, knowing us better than we know ourselves, has entrusted us with the message of reconciliation. Perhaps God might end a letter to us in the same way my grandfather closed his letter to my father before he took that first drive with his license: "A lot of responsibility to hand out, isn't it? A measure of the way we feel about you is that we're glad and proud to say, 'Take the car keys, and have a good time!'"

As we build up one another in our lives of prayer, in unending forgiveness for one another, and in the expansion of our Christ-centered and Spirit-enlivened imaginations, we just might find ourselves having the best time ever. Amen?

7

WHAT ARE WE STILL DOING HERE, PEOPLE?

With all of the joy, purpose, new life, and hope that result from being part of a community of faith shaped and defined by the biblical narrative of death and resurrection, the congregation of Grace Church (GC) is still a far cry from the vision of the new heaven and new earth John of Patmos is graced to see at the end of Revelation. In our life together, we are constantly amazed by the work of the Spirit among us. We laugh a whole lot together and dare to have fun in the ministry of Jesus Christ. We also continue to struggle and suffer. We've come a long way, *and* we've come to realize that for a community called and gathered in Christ's name on this side of Christ's return, our work together will never be done, and our experience of death will not end. This may sound like a complete downer to close out a book. But my hope, and the hope of the people of GC, is that by talking about some of the ways we're still going through the valley of the shadow of death, you and your congregation will be able to see that "going through it" is part of the journey. We, on our best days, have come to accept what we can never fix, what we'll never overcome, and what we must leave in Jesus's hands because it's too painful to even hope for. We continue to be a people rooted in God's perfect love and to receive God's amazing grace as we move forward into a future that only God knows and only God can create. We'll keep holding one another up as God holds us together, trying all the while to accept our status as an unsettled people. An unsettled, loved, and forgiven people is what we are, and I believe it's where the church universal will be for some time to come.

JUST WHEN I THOUGHT WE HAD IT FIGURED OUT

As I have mentioned several times in this book, the congregation of GC is located in a neighborhood with challenges. I am aware we are not unique in this. I'm a midwesterner, remember? We "pull ourselves up by our own bootstraps" and guard fiercely our privacy and independence. And I know that even though the pain is more hidden in some places, daily devastation is alive and well as nearly every household deals with something: addiction, broken relationships, family trauma, poverty, and the like. At the same time, we're all living in a world in turmoil, marked by systemic injustice, where violence against body, mind, and spirit is visited on millions daily. As you read the next story, it may sound a bit extreme. But remember, we're all experiencing our own hurts and devastations, and whatever suffering and brokenness your congregation is facing, you're not alone in it.

I'll begin by saying the violence and addiction in our neighborhood come in waves. That is, they're always there, but as a congregation we're only overwhelmed by them every couple of months or so. Those crushed souls using drugs on our property or leaving stolen property in our alley don't do it consistently. It ebbs and flows with the change of seasons and the location of dealers. One summer, the situation got particularly bad.

Ironically, and with some predictability, when things at church start firing on all cylinders and we're gliding on the grace of God, things in our neighborhood begin to tank. As a congregation that hadn't celebrated a baptism in quite some time, we were looking forward to welcoming a number of children and adults through the waters of Holy Baptism. In the course of our planning for this celebration, we realized we did not have enough baptismal candles. What a kick! We had to order baptismal candles! Hallelujah!

However, no one was at the church when the package of candles arrived. They were left outside our front door by the delivery company despite our repeated requests not to leave anything outside the church because delivered packages always grew legs. Before anyone from the congregation could pick them up, the candles were taken by a couple of desperate, unhoused neighbors who carried them to our alley and used them to cook heroin. The president of our congregation found the burned candles and spoons in the alley the next day.

We were shaken, angry, and desperately sad, to say the least. It was the last straw in a season of painful experiences. In the weeks leading up to the baptismal candle event, so many syringes had been left on our property that we decided we needed to close our playground. We couldn't risk the possibility that a child could accidentally come into contact with one. The kind gentleman who was paid pennies to check our property at night was running into the same folks camping out on the property over and over with escalating confrontations. The garbage left behind on our back stairs, including syringes and human waste, was piling up and unsafe for any member to dispose of. Of course, members did the work anyway. Our collective anxiety, anger, sadness, and frustration as a congregation was too much to carry quietly, so we decided to get together and talk about it.

In hindsight, I was more than a little unprepared for this meeting. In my mind, we had this! We knew how to have tough conversations as a congregation. We'd been doing it for years together. We could have Bible studies with all sorts of disagreements about fundamental differences in our understanding of who God is and how God is at work in the world. What I underestimated was the depth of pain and frustration and the feelings of powerlessness that our faith community carried. And with those deep feelings arose very different ways of dealing with our situation.

We decided to gather for an evening conversation. Each person present was given three minutes to talk. We agreed to use "I" statements and share what we were feeling along with what steps we thought should be taken. It didn't take long for me to see we were in for a long night. Some felt we had to lock down the property. Building bigger walls, adding more fencing, and not allowing our staff to answer the door were a few suggestions. We could not expose our congregation, and especially our youngest children, to this kind of risk. Others thought putting up firm barriers and refusing to answer the door would compromise our call to serve the least of these. "Should we not be about feeding the hungry and setting the prisoner free?" they asked. Others simply expressed their anger and frustration that no matter what we did, the situation never got any better. An old idea, to relocate the church, was laid before us.

We had determined at the outset of the meeting that we would take no longer than ninety minutes for this conversation. After eighty or so minutes, what had begun with my high hopes had given way to, as my husband describes it, a dumpster fire. Tears, red faces, crossed arms, and downcast eyes were all I could see. I had no idea what to do next, when one voice rang out from the group: "I guess the only thing we can do now is pray about it."

There it was. The voice of the Spirit broke into our sadness, anxiety, and anger. In that moment, everything changed. Don't get me wrong; we didn't fix the problem of drug use and poverty in our neighborhood. But God's presence filled the room. We all agreed to hold this situation in our prayers for two weeks. After that two-week period, we would come back together and talk about what we had heard from God. At the same time, we decided to take those two weeks to investigate, prayerfully, some ways we could begin to move forward by God's grace and provision to address the basic issue of safety. Moments before, the meeting had felt like a ship careening out of control toward a monstrous iceberg. Now light flooded the room, and we were cruising ahead together on the waters of the Spirit. Still, no one could have predicted what happened next.

Over the course of the next two weeks, our prayerful discernment led us to all sorts of resources. Our facilities team realized that a number of our outside lights were burned out, creating dark spaces around the perimeter of our property. They got to work immediately to change the bulbs. They also discussed the open staircase on the alley, decided it had become an attractive nuisance, and started getting bids to fence it in. We received training on the proper collection and disposal of syringes from a local nonprofit. They ran a needle exchange and were happy to provide us with grabbers, sharps containers, heavy gloves, and a disposal site for the syringes we collected. They even offered to clean everything up for us; we just had to give them a call. The bridge God built between our congregation and that nonprofit has led us to all sorts of opportunities for ministry together in our neighborhood. We renewed our relationship with our local police division. They were happy to increase patrols in our neighborhood during the late-night and early morning hours. We also developed closer relationships with our immediate neighbors as we encouraged one another in our desire to work for common goals and establish clear boundaries with our unhoused neighbors.

When we came back together, we couldn't believe how God had been working. We shared with one another all we had accomplished together and spoke about our renewed sense of being called to be about God's love and light where God had placed us. No one knew what the future might bring, but we were committed, together, to building one another up and building up the neighborhood around us that God loved so much. But for me, the most miraculous outcome of the whole experience was that no one left the congregation.

Nobody got everything they wanted. Those who wanted us to build bigger walls saw the fence put up around the staircase in the alley, but that was a far cry from locking down the whole property. Those who felt passionately that we needed to serve the least of these knew we were moving forward with a stronger police presence and clearer boundaries for those who spent time on our property even as we continued in our resolve to answer the door for anyone in need. Those who wanted to relocate knew we weren't going anywhere but that we were going to renew our commitment to be in relationship with our closest neighbors. Anyone from that meeting could have said, "I've had it. The group didn't do what I thought was best, so I'm out." We all know how often that happens. But no one did.

After that event, the syringes didn't disappear and the problems weren't fixed. And yet, God brought us closer together, renewed our sense of purpose in the neighborhood, and reminded us of the power we did have to serve with more intentionality and to create a safer community. Would this all have happened if we weren't being shaped by the word of God that brings us through death to resurrection over and over again? Maybe, but I doubt it. We were walking through the valley of the shadow of death, *and* goodness and mercy were following us all along the way.

DEATH AND RESURRECTION IS THE WAY OF THE CHURCH

I just love that story. I love it because at the end, GC didn't fix the problems we were facing in the course of our ministry and life together. It isn't a story of one congregation facing the problems of poverty, drug addiction, hopelessness, and the like and "saving" the neighborhood (whatever that might mean). It is a story of God doing God's project—thy will be done—in and through one congregation. *God* is doing the work of saving and restoring, of creating new life and bringing about resurrection. The people of GC and the wider community were gifted with some hope and healing experiences not because the church figured it all out and fixed it but because the people let it be God's project and then took the small steps along the way they were led by God to take. They made it about building one another up instead of being right or wrong. They looked to God's guidance and decided to take God's direction wherever it would lead. I'm so grateful I got to be a part of it.

The way of death and resurrection is not the way of daily triumph, at least not ours. God overcomes daily what we cannot in and through Christ, but resurrection is from God and for the sake of the world. As we continue to be the church, shaped and empowered by this message, we're not going to win a lot of medals. It's not going to be one day of perfect, Christ-centered bliss after another. We'll often find ourselves feeling as if we're on a ship careening out of control, unable to avoid a collision with the iceberg immediately before us. And somehow, God will keep finding a way to resurrect us even, especially when we cannot see that resurrection is possible. God's desire is for our life, our joy, and our thriving in the world, even as we await the fulfillment of all God's promises in Christ Jesus.

In the years following the baptismal candle fiasco and still today, we continue to suffer alongside our neighborhood. As I write this, nearly all of the windows in my office and the office of the church administrator are broken. An unhoused neighbor struggling with mental illness and addiction became frustrated about his life and threw rocks at them. We haven't fixed them yet, not only because they're expensive but because he might just come back and throw some more rocks.

We are not the pretty church, the musical church, the church with all of the young families, or the social justice church. We are the church called and gathered in the name of Jesus Christ, and we are shaped by God's story. The biblical narrative tells us who we are as beloved children of God. That story changes us from the inside out and empowers us to be who God wants us to be in our neighborhood for the sake of the world.

Further, as a church leader, it is impossible for me to communicate fully how empowering it is to serve a congregation that understands itself as formed by the biblical narrative of death and resurrection. As we serve together, the people of GC remind me daily that *I am formed* by God's story of death and resurrection too. I am a child of God serving alongside other children of God (1 John 3:1), who are called together and made new by the power of the Holy Spirit (1 John 4:13). At the same time, finding our identity together in Scripture makes clear what my pastoral role is. Yes, I write newsletter articles, cultivate relationships in the congregation and in the community, participate in board meetings, and so forth. But through it all, I am directed by the people of GC to look at everything we're doing through the lens of the identity we have been given in the biblical narrative—the lens of new life, death, and resurrection. Church council meetings are necessary. The early church held them and did its best to arrive prayerfully at the most faithful decisions (Acts 15). However, God's people were also instructed to continue the work of Jesus: "Very truly, I tell you, the one who believes in me will also do the works that I do and, in fact, will do greater works than these" (John 14:12). If pastors, and congregations, are constantly in meetings, doing administrative tasks, or arguing about the budget and Sunday school curriculum, are we living our identity as children of God called to lift up the lowly and fill the hungry with good things (Ps 107:9; Luke 1:53)?

Similarly, the Bible is not only able to guide leaders as we discern together with congregations our roles and the use of our time and energy; it has much to say about the reality of congregational conflict. Is conflict a pervasive experience of life together? The biblical narrative says, "Yes!" (Gal 1:6–9). We need not be worried when conflict arises that somehow we're doing it wrong. Disagreements about our work and life together have been a part of the church experience from the very beginning. However, *how* we disagree with one another must also be shaped by God's word. We must not be a people who allow the sun to go down on our anger (Eph 4:26) or refuse to work for the building up of the body of Christ (Eph 4:12). We are who the biblical narrative says we are. We will disagree about what direction God is calling us as we are formed by this narrative, *and* we will continue to engage with the narrative prayerfully, knowing we see in a mirror dimly. As the apostle Paul declares, "Now I know only in part; then I will know fully, even as I have been fully known" (1 Cor 13:12). We will fail because we cannot know the mind of God, even as we're doing our very best to keep up with the Holy Spirit. But we trust God will be faithful to us as God has been faithful to God's people from generation to generation (Ps 145:4). With my role clarified, I have confidence to lead the congregation I serve into the death and resurrection that is constant in our lives of faith: "For if we have been united with [Christ] in a death like his, we will certainly be united with him in a resurrection like his" (Rom 6:5).

Here and now, in a time often marked by blame, panic, and despair, God has given us an opportunity to thrive. Thriving in this time of confusion will not come of our own resourcefulness, problem-solving skills, practicality, or creativity. Thriving will come as the Holy Spirit moves us to surrender to the reality that our very survival as individuals and as the church is determined by God alone. Once the gift of surrender comes, we may live freely, boldly, and dare I say joyfully in Christ's way of death and resurrection, completely dependent upon God's promise to resurrect us over and over again. Here we live within the biblical narrative throughout which God declares unflinchingly that God's steadfast love and faithfulness endure forever. Here we move as God's beloved children who *receive* our identity from the one who creates and sustains us. Here we have our being as a people called and gathered in Christ's name to love God and our neighbor in whatever way *God* leads us. Our life together is a constant adventure in the Spirit!

ONE MORE BIBLE STORY

I used to loathe preaching on the transfiguration. That's the fancy name for the story in Matthew, Mark, and Luke in which Jesus goes up the mountain with a couple of his disciples and appears to them in dazzling white clothes alongside Moses and Elijah. I never liked that passage because so few of us have had such beautiful and powerful visions of Jesus. Sure, some lucky folks get glimpses of the divine with this heavenly aura. Some are even bold enough to tell others about it. But most of us haven't seen such a wonder. We live out our callings at the base of the mountain with the other disciples who weren't invited, wishing we were somehow good enough to have been welcomed up there for the vision too.

But last year, I understood this passage from Scripture and its significance for *all* the disciples in a different way. I wish I could say it was my own brilliant insight, but I'm pretty sure I got it from someone else. You see, in all three Gospels, this story of Jesus's glorious transformation comes immediately on the heels of two teachings from Jesus that must have been devastating for the disciples:

1. "The Son of Man must undergo great suffering, and be rejected by the elders, chief priests, and scribes, and be killed, and on the third day be raised." (Luke 9:22)
2. "If any want to become my followers, let them deny themselves and take up their cross daily and follow me. For those who want to save their life will lose it, and those who lose their life for my sake will save it." (Luke 9:23–24)

How would you have felt after hearing those teachings? We know Christ Jesus on this side of the resurrection, and it is still hard to hear those words. Imagine if you were the disciples, having given up everything to follow this Jesus, and you heard he was going to be killed and you were in for a rough time too. Might you have wanted to bail at that point? I certainly would! I still want to bail from time to time.

Life in the faith community and as a follower of Jesus Christ, as I have described it, is not exactly the stuff of recruiting posters. Yes, in relationship with God, resurrection *always* follows death. However, death is still a prerequisite for resurrection, and nearly all of us would rather not accept death as part of the deal. The first disciples had to be crushed by Jesus's statements of the truth, and frankly, so am I on more days than I'd like to admit. But God does not distinguish between the really committed disciples, those willing to walk into a den of lions and accept the consequences, and those who are faint of heart. God is determined to give us—all of us—the reassurance and hope we need to keep walking this road of discipleship when the crosses of life come to us.

So what does this have to do with Jesus's transfiguration? God knows we have our work cut out for us in loving God and loving the world, and so did the first disciples. So when life got overwhelming and they wondered if they were following the right guy, Jesus took a few of them—just enough to be able to share their story with the rest convincingly—up a mountain, and God showed them what they needed to see. God spoke to the disciples directly and said, "This is my Son, my Chosen; listen to him!" (Luke 9:35b). In other words, God said, "Keep going! You're following the right guy! Even when it sounds and feels like everything's gone off the rails, don't despair! I promise I'll see you through this to resurrection and new life!"

OK, Luke's version was much more succinct than mine, but the beautiful, grace-filled Gospel remains. When you feel like you want to give up because you just don't know if you can keep going on this difficult road of death and resurrection, remember this: You're going the right way! You're following the Son of God who rose on the third day! God will see you through whatever it is you're facing and bring you to resurrection and new life!

God has told us who we are as communities of faith. For all of our fear, anger, and desire for control, we are God's beloved children. The incredibly good news is that God has been in loving relationship with, guided, spoken to, and provided for flawed people—just like those of us who make up our congregations—from generation to generation. And right here, in our confusion and uncertainty about what the future will bring, we are given a glorious opportunity. We are released from finding the "right answers," following rigid mission plans, and maintaining what always has been. God calls us, as God's people, to engage the biblical narrative in such a way that we are remade as God's dependents, instruments of God's will for life, healing, forgiveness, and reconciliation. We are made to respond to what God is doing and where God is moving. We are made to enter into the new life God is bringing about. And when we experience the grief that necessarily comes with death, we may cry out to our Creator and Redeemer with the honesty and boldness of lament, confident that God will work resurrection in God's time.

We are free to follow our Lord and Savior Jesus Christ as a people belonging to God. We stumble and God picks us up. We experience joy in the work of the Spirit, and God celebrates with us. We are beloved of God, called to continue the work God revealed to us in Jesus. So let's get to it! Amen?!

Thanks be to God! Amen.

NOTES

Chapter 1

1 All proper names have been changed to protect anonymity.
2 Rachael J. Powell, "Thriving in Disorientation: How Preaching the Biblical Narrative Shapes and Empowers Christian Community" (DMin diss., Luther Seminary, 2019), 73.
3 Powell, 71.
4 Powell, 78–79.

Chapter 2

1 Hayyim Angel, "Biblical Prayers and Rabbinic Responses: Balancing Truthfulness and Respect before God," *Jewish Bible Quarterly* 38, no. 1 (2010): 3.
2 Jon D. Levenson, *Creation and the Persistence of Evil: The Jewish Drama of Divine Omnipotence* (Princeton, NJ: Princeton University Press, 1988), 17.

Chapter 4

1 Rolf A. Jacobson, "We Are Our Stories: Narrative Dimension of Human Identity and Its Implications for Christian Faith Formation," *Word & World* 34, no. 2 (2014): 123–24.
2 Paul Ricœur, *Time and Narrative*, vol. 1, trans. Kathleen McLaughlin and David Pellauer (Chicago: University of Chicago Press, 1984); Paul Ricœur, *Time and Narrative*, vol. 2, trans. Kathleen McLaughlin and David Pellauer (Chicago: University of Chicago Press, 1986); Paul Ricœur, *Time and Narrative*, vol. 3, trans. Kathleen Blamey and David Pellauer (Chicago: University of Chicago Press, 1988).
3 Ricœur, 1:34.

4 Ricœur, 1:20.
5 Ricœur, 1:21–22. I am risking here a profound oversimplification of Aristotle and Ricœur's arguments. The aim is briefly to set a foundation.
6 Ricœur, 1:21.
7 Ricœur, 3:101. See chapters 6 and 7 for Ricœur's full discussion.
8 Ricœur, 1:38.
9 Ricœur, 1:41.
10 Ricœur, 1:41.
11 Ricœur, 1:52–82.
12 Ricœur, 1:54.
13 Ricœur, 1:60.
14 Ricœur, 1:64.
15 Ricœur, 1:66.
16 Ricœur, 1:72.
17 Ricœur, 1:76.
18 Emmanuel Katongole and Jonathan Wilson-Hartgrove, *Mirror to the Church: Resurrecting Faith after Genocide in Rwanda* (Grand Rapids, MI: Zondervan, 2009).
19 Katongole and Wilson-Hartgrove, 67–68.
20 Katongole and Wilson-Hartgrove, 84–85.

Chapter 5

1 The following quotes are taken from my doctoral work. In order to gather data about the preacher's role in the development of congregational identity, it was necessary I ask GC members about my proclamation. What follows are a few of the responses. For the complete list of questions posed to GC members, please see Powell, "Thriving in Disorientation," appendix B, "Follow-Up Questions to Initial Interviews."
2 Powell, 83.
3 Powell, 92.
4 Powell, 85.
5 Powell, 88–89.
6 Powell, 89.
7 Richard Lischer, *The End of Words: The Language of Reconciliation in a Culture of Violence*, Lyman Beecher Lectures in Preaching (Grand Rapids, MI: William B. Eerdmans, 2005), 96.

RECOMMENDED RESOURCES

PRIMER PACKAGE

All you and your congregation need to get centered in the biblical narrative, prayer, and the posture of responding to the movement of the Holy Spirit.

McLaren, Brian D. *We Make the Road by Walking: A Year-Long Quest for Spiritual Formation, Reorientation, and Activation.* New York: Jericho Books, 2014.

In one book, McLaren will lead you through the arc of the biblical narrative with plenty of reflection material for great conversation. Agree or disagree with his conclusions as you place them together with the biblical text. This was the book that the people of Grace Church committed to reading with me alongside the Bible for one year. It was the Spirit-filled launchpad for our continuing commitment to meet weekly for prayer and study.

Reese, Martha Grace. *Unbinding the Gospel: Real Life Evangelism.* 2nd ed. Unbinding the Gospel Series: Church Leaders' Study. St. Louis: Chalice, 2008.

The most important passages from this text, for our congregation, were those that laid out processes through which we were invited to share with one another our experiences of God and led into prayer for and with one another. I cannot overstate the significance of her process of "prayer triads" as described in this book. In a very short period of time, we were able to move from a congregation that cared deeply for each other to one that entered fully into one another's lives. We found ourselves carrying one another's burdens and celebrating together as a community rooted in the love of God in Christ.

Zscheile, Dwight J. *Agile Church: Spirit-Led Innovation in an Uncertain Age.* New York: Morehouse, 2014.

When the Spirit tells your congregation to move, how quickly are you able to respond? We have discovered that when we pray and study Scripture together, the Spirit opens up all sorts of opportunities for us to be a part of what God is doing in the world. It may be a phone call from a mission partner or a "chance" conversation with a neighbor, but once the idea has been planted, it can grow quickly. Zscheile's book has helped us develop our ability to respond to the Spirit's guidance *and* create avenues of faith learning from our false starts and missteps.

THE POWER OF LAMENT

These texts give readers deep explorations of our necessity as the people of God to cry out to God when we're hurting.

Levenson, Jon D. *Creation and the Persistence of Evil: The Jewish Drama of Divine Omnipotence.* Princeton, NJ: Princeton University Press, 1988.

This one's for the hard-core theology lover. Levenson is a brilliant academic and takes the reader through God's persistent commitment to love and sustain all of creation. This passage from his first chapter provides a taste of his emphatic writing: "The survival of ordered reality hangs only upon God's vigilance. . . . Creation endures because God has pledged in an eternal covenant that it shall endure" (p. 17). How's that for a response to our cries of lament?

Rah, Soong-Chan. *Prophetic Lament: A Call for Justice in Troubled Times*. Downers Grove, IL: InterVarsity, 2015.

Before my doctoral studies at Luther, I had not heard of Rah. His theological background is different from mine, which only added to my appreciation for this book. Rah does not hesitate to critique his experience of church life and, from his perspective, his tradition's refusal to name the suffering inherent in being God's people for the sake of the world. This read is not for the faint of heart (it takes the reader through the pain of Lamentations) and is one that has encouraged me to be more open about the sufferings we endure as God's people in a broken and hurting world.

Stulman, Louis. "Reading the Prophets as Meaning-Making Literature for Communities Under Siege." *Horizons in Biblical Theology* 29, no. 2 (2007): 153–75.

If academic articles are more your speed, Stulman's work is for you. For congregations enduring one struggle after the next, he offers the Prophets as the place to start again. His argument that through lament God leads people to a place of restored purpose is about as inspiring as it gets. He also talks about how the prophetic witness is "survival literature" given to those who remain after catastrophe strikes. Describing many who are left in the church today as "survivors" rings true to my experience.

NARRATIVE SHAPES IDENTITY

These books and this article offer a much deeper dive into the discussions surrounding the power of narrative to shape identity. If you're interested at all in learning more, I highly recommend them.

Brown, Warren S., and Brad D. Strawn. *The Physical Nature of Christian Life: Neuroscience, Psychology, and the Church*. Cambridge: Cambridge University Press, 2012.

The title says it all. It is written by two authors, one a psychologist and one a theologian. They each contribute wisdom from their respective fields and determine together the fundamental role narrative plays in the development of self. The section entitled "Stories We Live By" is most instructive for pastors, preachers, and all congregational leaders.

Katongole, Emmanuel. *The Sacrifice of Africa: A Political Theology for Africa*. Eerdmans Ekklesia Series. Grand Rapids: W. B. Eerdmans, 2011.

Need more inspiration for holding, every day, to the biblical narrative as that which forms our identity? Here it is. Katongole provides a number of examples of individuals whose lives are determined by their status as beloved children of God and their insistence that they are called to live that identity for the sake of the world. These stories of radical forgiveness and boldly active peacemaking are food for the soul.

Katongole, Emmanuel, and Jonathan Wilson-Hartgrove. *Mirror to the Church: Resurrecting Faith after Genocide in Rwanda*. Grand Rapids: Zondervan, 2009.

If you want practical applications for the power of narrative to shape identity, no one can provide them better than

Katongole. This book is an easy read and hard to get through. In very plain English, he lays out the failings of the Christian church in Rwanda to proclaim the biblical narrative as *the formative narrative* for followers of Jesus Christ with disastrous consequences. It is not only a tragic cautionary tale but a call to all congregations to evaluate what is most important to us.

Ricœur, Paul. "Listening to the Parables of Jesus. Text: Matthew 13:31–32 and 45–46." *Criterion* 13 (1974): 18–22.
     If my grossly oversimplified version of Ricœur's philosophy left you dry, here's a great article to give you Ricœur's own biblical application of how it is that narrative shapes identity. It's short and sweet and may just change the way you read and/or preach from the gift of the biblical narrative.

BOOKS TOO BEAUTIFUL TO MISS

Maybe you've already been introduced to these books. If you have, thanks be to God! If not, read them. You won't regret it.

Brueggemann, Walter. *The Practice of Prophetic Imagination: Preaching an Emancipating Word.* Minneapolis: Fortress, 2012.
     In my humble opinion, this is one of the best books ever written on the practice and call of preaching. However, it is also for any child of God who wants their mind blown by the beauty, honesty, and inspiration available to us in the biblical narrative. It's just that good.

Davis, Ellen F. *Getting Involved with God: Rediscovering the Old Testament.* Cambridge: Cowley, 2001.
     Davis takes readers through the literature of the Old Testament and reacquaints them with the God who desires intimate

relationship with each and every one of us. Her discussion of the Song of Songs is worth the read in itself.

Rupp, Joyce. *Praying Our Goodbyes: A Spiritual Companion through Life's Losses and Sorrows.* **Notre Dame: Ave Maria, 1988.**

This book brings it all together—prayer, lament, and the biblical narrative—and is ready-made for congregational conversation. Rupp offers a compassionate, direct, and faithful approach to acknowledging and moving forward through the constant losses we face as beloved children of God. It is truly the reader's gift to themselves to read it.